GRADE 6

Common Core Mathematics

Practice at 3 Levels ●●●

Table of Contents

D1379386

Using This Book

What Is the Common Core?

The Common Core State Standards are an initiative by the states to set shared, consistent, and clear expectations of what students are expected to learn, so teachers and parents know what they need to do to help them. The standards are designed to be rigorous and pertinent to the real world. They reflect the knowledge and skills that our young people need for success in college and careers.

What Are the Intended Outcomes of Common Core?

The goal of the Common Core Standards is to facilitate the following competencies.

Students will:
- demonstrate independence;
- build strong content knowledge;
- respond to the varying demands of audience, task, purpose, and discipline;
- comprehend as well as critique;
- value evidence;
- use technology and digital media strategically and capably;
- come to understand other perspectives and cultures.

What Does This Mean for You?

If your state has joined the Common Core State Standards Initiative, then as a teacher you are required to incorporate these standards into your lesson plans. Your students may need targeted practice in order to meet grade-level standards and expectations and thereby be promoted to the next grade. This book is appropriate for on-grade-level students as well as intervention, ELs, struggling readers, and special needs. To see if your state has joined the initiative, visit the Common Core States Standards Initiative website to view the most recent adoption map: http://www.corestandards.org/in-the-states.

What Does the Common Core Say Specifically About Math?

For math, the Common Core sets the following key expectations.

- Make sense of problems and persevere in solving them.
- Reason abstractly and quantitatively.
- Construct viable arguments and critique the reasoning of others.
- Model with mathematics.
- Use appropriate tools strategically.
- Attend to precision.
- Look for and make use of structure.
- Look for and express regularity in repeated reasoning.

How Does Common Core Mathematics Help My Students?

- **Mini-lesson for each unit** introduces
  Common Core math skills and concepts.

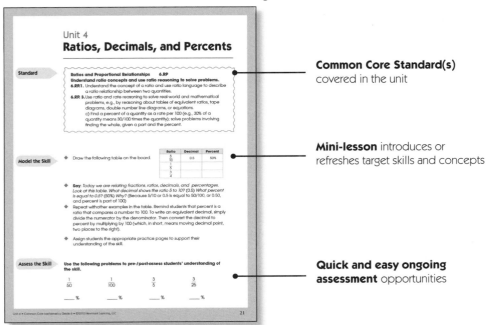

Common Core Standard(s)
covered in the unit

Mini-lesson introduces or
refreshes target skills and concepts

**Quick and easy ongoing
assessment** opportunities

- **Four practice pages** with three levels of differentiated practice,
  and word problems follow each mini-lesson.

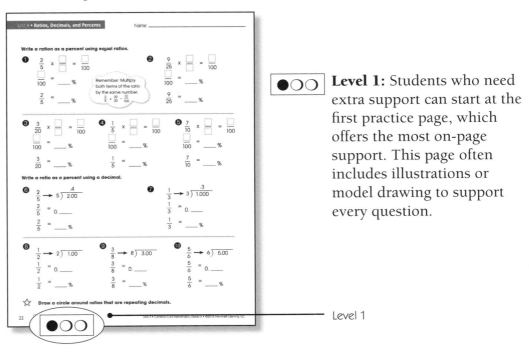

Level 1: Students who need
extra support can start at the
first practice page, which
offers the most on-page
support. This page often
includes illustrations or
model drawing to support
every question.

Level 1

Level 2: The second level of practice offers streamlined support features for the first few problems (illustrations, model drawing, or an algorithm reminder for support).

☆ Each practice page includes a bonus thinking-skills question so students can answer "How do you know?" to address Common Core Standards of Mathematical Practice and demonstrate their reasoning and understanding of the concept.

☆ How do you write the ratio $\frac{3}{8}$ as a percent? Explain the steps you take.

Bonus Thinking Skills question on each practice page

Level 3: The third practice page does not offer on-page support and depicts how students are expected to be able to perform at this grade level, whether in class or in testing.

Word Problems: Each unit ends with a page of short-answer and multiple-choice word problems so students are challenged to marry their computation skills with their quantitative-reasoning and problem-solving skills and grow more familiar with the types of problems they will encounter on standardized tests.

Word Problem Page

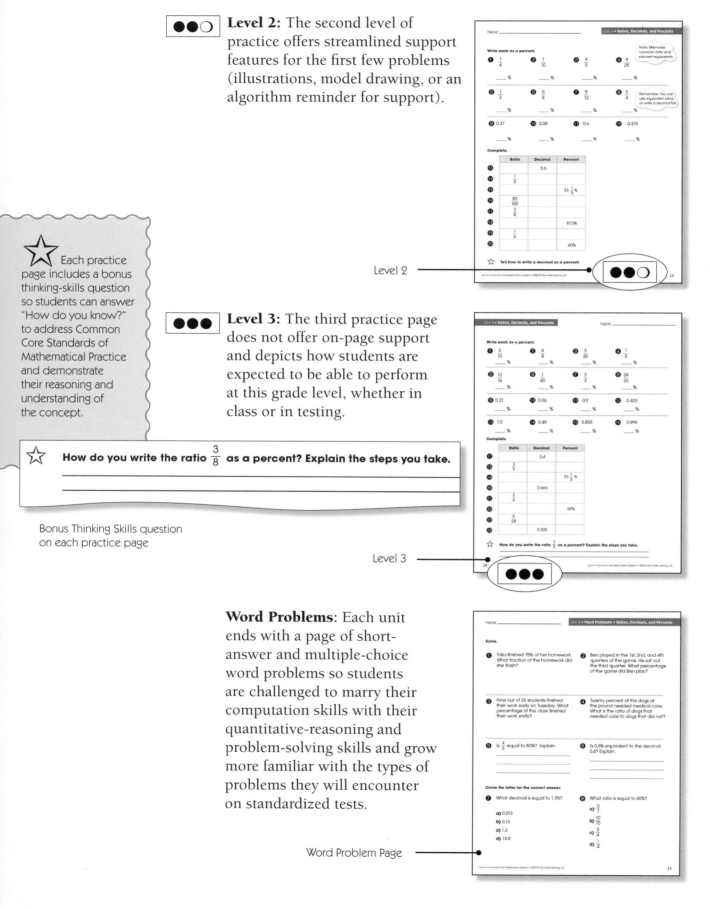

Common Core Standards Alignment Chart • Grade 6

Units	6.RP.1	6.RP.2	6.RP.3	6.NS.1	6.NS.2	6.NS.3	6.NS.4	6.NS.5	6.NS.6	6.NS.7	6.NS.8	6.EE.1	6.EE.2	6.EE.3	6.EE.4	6.EE.5	6.EE.6	6.EE.7	6.EE.8	6.EE.9	6.G.1	6.G.2	6.G.3	6.G.4	6.SP.1	6.SP.2	6.SP.3	6.SP.4	6.SP.5
Ratios & Proportional Relationships																													
Unit 1: Ratios & Equivalent Ratios	✔		✔																										
Unit 2: Rates		✔	✔																										
Unit 3: Understand Percent	✔		✔																										
Unit 4: Ratios, Decimals, and Percents	✔		✔																										
Unit 5: Find Percent of a Number			✔																										
The Number System																													
Unit 6: Divide Whole Numbers					✔																								
Unit 7: Add and Subtract Decimals						✔																							
Unit 8: Multiply and Divide Decimals						✔																							
Unit 9: Greatest Common Factor & Least Common Multiple							✔																						
Unit 10: Multiply Fractions				✔																									
Unit 11: Divide Fractions				✔																									
Unit 12: Understand Integers								✔		✔																			
Unit 13: Order Rational Numbers									✔	✔																			
Unit 14: Graph Points on the Coordinate Plane									✔		✔																		
Expressions & Equations																													
Unit 15: Exponents												✔																	
Unit 16: Order of Operations												✔																	
Unit 17: Algebraic Expressions													✔																
Unit 18: Properties of Operations														✔	✔														
Unit 19: Write and Solve Equations																✔	✔	✔											
Unit 20: Write and Solve Inequalities																✔			✔										
Unit 21: Graph Equations																				✔									
Geometry																													
Unit 22: Area of Polygons																					✔								
Unit 23: Draw Polygons on the Coordinate Plane																							✔						
Unit 24: Find Surface Area																								✔					
Unit 25: Find Volume																						✔							
Statistics & Probability																													
Unit 26: Mean, Median, and Mode																									✔	✔	✔		
Unit 27: Make and Interpret Dot Pots																												✔	✔
Unit 28: Make and Interpret Histograms																												✔	✔
Unit 29: Make and Interpret Box Plots																												✔	✔

Unit 1
Ratios and Equivalent Ratios

Ratios & Proportional Relationships
Understand ratio concepts and use ratio reasoning to solve problems.
6.RP.1. Understand the concept of a ratio and use ratio language to describe a ratio relationship between two quantities.
6.RP.3. Use ratio and rate reasoning to solve real-world and mathematical problems, e.g., by reasoning about tables of equivalent ratios, tape diagrams, double number line diagrams, or equations.

Model the Skill

◆ Draw the following model on the board.

◆ **Say**: *Today we are going to be finding ratios and equivalent ratios. A ratio shows the relative sizes of two or more values. Ratios can be shown in different ways. A fraction is one way to show a ratio. Look at the circles in this array. Three of the twelve circles are shaded. Write a fraction that shows how many ($\frac{3}{12}$).*

◆ Explain to students that another way to express 3/12 is 3:12 or 3 to 12. Then ask students to think of a way to simplify the expression by writing an equivalent ratio.

$$\frac{3}{12} \quad = \quad 3:12 \quad = \quad 3 \text{ to } 12$$

$$\frac{3}{12} \quad = \quad \frac{1}{4} \quad = \quad 1:4 \quad = \quad 1 \text{ to } 4$$

◆ Assign students the appropriate practice pages to support their understanding of the skill.

Assess the Skill

Use the following problems to pre-/post-assess students' understanding of the skill.

◆ Ask students to use the model below to find the following ratios:

□□□□
△△△△△
○○○○○○

□'s to △'s =
□'s to ○'s =
△'s to shapes =

○'s to shapes =
○'s to □'s + △'s=
□'s to ○'s + △'s =

Unit 2
Rates

Ratios & Proportional Relationships
Understand ratio concepts and use ratio reasoning to solve problems.

6.RP.2. Understand the concept of a unit rate a/b associated with a ratio a:b with b≠0, and use rate language in the context of a ratio relationship. For example, "This recipe has a ratio of 3 cups of flour to 4 cups of sugar, so there is 3/4 cup of flour for each cup of sugar." "We paid $75 for 15 hamburgers, which is a rate of $5 per hamburger."

6.RP. 3. Use ratio and rate reasoning to solve real-world and mathematical problems, e.g., by reasoning about tables of equivalent ratios, tape diagrams, double number line diagrams, or equations.

Model the Skill

◆ Draw the following rates and model on the board.

rate	unit rate
$33/11 lb.	$3/1 lb.
60 mi/2 hr	30 mi/1 hr
6 triangles/3 circles	2 triangles/1 circle

◆ **Say**: *A rate is a ratio that compares two quantities of different increments, or units. For example, 33 dollars for 11 lbs of fruit is a rate. 60 miles per two hours is also a rate. A unit rate reduces the rate so that the denominator is 1. $3 per pound is a unit rate. 30 miles per hour is a unit rate. 6 triangles per 3 circles can be reduced to a unit rate. What is the unit rate in this model?* (2 triangles per 1 circle, or 2/1, or 2:1)

◆ Assign students the appropriate practice pages to support their understanding of the skill.

Assess the Skill

Use the following problems to pre-/post-assess students' understanding of the skill.

4 for $32.00

rate: 4 : _____

unit rate: _____ : _____

rate: 30 km/hr

time: 5.5 hours

Distance: _____

Distance: 360 miles

rate: 15 mph

time: _____

Name _____

Use equivalent ratios. Find the unit rate.

1 ○ ○ ○ ○
△ △ △ △
△ △ △ △

●	1	4	
▲		8	

rate   8 : 4

unit rate ____ : 1

2 30 miles in 5 hours

rate   30 : ____

unit rate ____ : 1

____ mph

> Miles per hour is a rate.

---

3 3 for $21.00

rate   3 : ____

unit rate ____ : ____

4 36 inches in 3 feet

rate   ____ : ____

unit rate ▯
              ▔
            ▯

Use the formula Distance = rate x time (D = rt) to complete the chart.

	Distance	rate (speed)	time
5	_____ miles	25 mph	3 h
6	_____ kilometers	14 kph	4 h
7	_____ feet	6 ft per sec	2 sec
8	42 miles	_____ mph	7 h
9	256 miles	40 mph	____ h
10	60 km	30 kph	____ h
11	90 km	40 kph	____ h
12	_____	20 kph	8 h
13	_____	30 kph	3 h
14	100 miles	_____	4 h

☆ **Look at the chart. Did you divide to solve some problems? Draw a circle around those problems.**

Name _____

Solve.

1 Look at the sale prices. Which is the better buy? How much does one can cost?

SALE
5 for $1.00

SALE
12 for $3.00

2 Find and compare the unit prices. Which one is the better buy?

SALE
3 for $1.00

SALE
10 for $3.00

3 The diner sells bagels for $0.75 each. The bagel shop sells 1 dozen for $7.00. Which is the better buy?

4 The fisherman is selling salmon for $7.99/lb. The supermarket has 2-lb packages of salmon for $14.98. Which is a better buy?

5 Cheyenne drove 3,000 miles in 75 hours. At this rate, how long will it take her to drive 4,000 miles?

6 The factory makes 400 cars per day. If the workday is eight hours long, what is the hourly rate at which cars are produced?

Circle the letter for the correct answer.

7 A potter makes 6 bowls in 3 hours. How long would it take the potter to make 14 bowls?

a) 6 hours
b) 7 hours
c) 8 hours
d) 9 hours

8 The mechanic does 4 oil changes in 2 hours. How many oil changes can the mechanic do in 8 hours?

a) 2 oil changes
b) 4 oil changes
c) 10 oil changes
d) 16 oil changes

Unit 3
Understand Percent

Standard

Ratios & Proportional Relationships
Understand ratio concepts and use ratio reasoning to solve problems.
6.RP.1. Understand the concept of a ratio and use ratio language to describe a ratio relationship between two quantities.
6.RP.3. Use ratio and rate reasoning to solve real-world and mathematical problems, e.g., by reasoning about tables of equivalent ratios, tape diagrams, double number line diagrams, or equations.
    c) Find a percent of a quantity as a rate per 100 (e.g., 30% of a quantity means 30/100 times the quantity); solve problems involving finding the whole, given a part and the percent.

Model the Skill

◆ Draw the following models on the board.

◆ **Say**: *Today we are going to be finding percent. A percentage shows the rate per 100. For example, if 40 out of 100 people are wearing white socks, the portion of people wearing white socks would be 40/100, or 40 per 100, therefore 40% of the people are wearing white socks.*

◆ **Say**: *Look at the models. What fraction does each model show? What percent does each model show?*

◆ Assign students the appropriate practice pages to support their understanding of the skill.

Assess the Skill

Use the following problems to pre-/post-assess students' understanding of the skill.

Write each percent to describe each shaded part.

1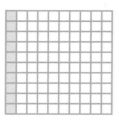

_____

2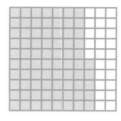

_____

3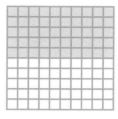

_____

4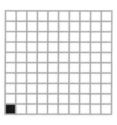

_____

5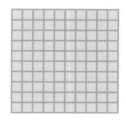

_____

6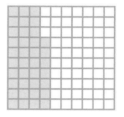

_____

Write each ratio as a decimal and a percent.

7 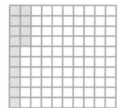 $\dfrac{14}{100}$

decimal _____

percent _____

8 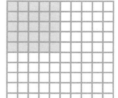 $\dfrac{25}{100}$

decimal _____

percent _____

9 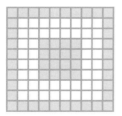 $\dfrac{52}{100}$

decimal _____

percent _____

10  $\dfrac{3}{10}$

decimal _____

percent _____

   Draw a circle around the model that shows 25% *not* shaded.

Name _____

Write a percent to describe each shaded part.

1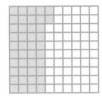

2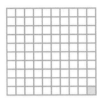

3

_____   _____   _____

4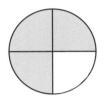

5

Remember: Percent is a ratio that compares a number to 100. Write an equivalent ratio $\frac{3}{10} = \frac{\square}{100}$

_____   _____

Write each ratio as a decimal and a percent.

6 $\dfrac{50}{100}$ **7** $\dfrac{65}{100}$ **8** $\dfrac{3}{100}$ **9** $\dfrac{8}{100}$

____ ____   ____ ____   ____ ____   ____ ____

10 $\dfrac{1}{2}$ **11** $\dfrac{12}{100}$ **12** $\dfrac{5}{100}$ **13** $\dfrac{42}{100}$

____ ____   ____ ____   ____ ____   ____ ____

14 $\dfrac{1}{100}$ **15** $\dfrac{7}{100}$ **16** $\dfrac{58}{100}$ **17** $\dfrac{23}{100}$

____ ____   ____ ____   ____ ____   ____ ____

18 $\dfrac{9}{100}$ **19** $\dfrac{15}{100}$ **20** $\dfrac{4}{100}$ **21** $\dfrac{3}{4}$

____ ____   ____ ____   ____ ____   ____ ____

 Tell what 110% means. Draw a picture.

Unit 4
Ratios, Decimals, and Percents

Standard

Ratios & Proportional Relationships
Understand ratio concepts and use ratio reasoning to solve problems.
6.RP.1. Understand the concept of a ratio and use ratio language to describe a ratio relationship between two quantities.
6.RP.3. Use ratio and rate reasoning to solve real-world and mathematical problems, e.g., by reasoning about tables of equivalent ratios, tape diagrams, double number line diagrams, or equations.
c) Find a percent of a quantity as a rate per 100 (e.g., 30% of a quantity means 30/100 times the quantity); solve problems involving finding the whole, given a part and the percent.

Model the Skill

◆ Draw the following table on the board.

Ratio	Decimal	Percent
$\frac{5}{10}$	0.5	50%
$\frac{1}{5}$		
$\frac{3}{4}$		

◆ **Say**: *Today we are relating fractions, ratios, decimals, and percentages. Look at this table. What decimal shows the ratio 5 to 10?* (0.5) *What percent is equal to 0.5?* (50%) *Why?* (Because 5/10 or 0.5 is equal to 50/100, or 0.50, and percent is part of 100)

◆ Repeat with other examples in the table. Remind students that percent is a ratio that compares a number to 100. To write an equivalent decimal, simply divide the numerator by the denominator. Then convert the decimal to percent by multiplying by 100 (which, in short, means moving the decimal point two places to the right).

◆ Assign students the appropriate practice pages to support their understanding of the skill.

Assess the Skill

Use the following problems to pre-/post-assess students' understanding of the skill.

$\frac{1}{50}$ $\frac{1}{100}$ $\frac{3}{5}$ $\frac{3}{25}$

_____ %   _____ %   _____ %   _____ %

Name _____

Write a ratio as a percent using equal ratios.

1 $\dfrac{2}{5}$ x $\dfrac{\square}{\square}$ = $\dfrac{\square}{100}$

$\dfrac{\square}{100}$ = ____ %

$\dfrac{2}{5}$ = ____ %

Remember: Multiply both terms of the ratio by the same number.
$\dfrac{2}{5}$ x $\dfrac{20}{20}$ = $\dfrac{\blacksquare}{100}$

2 $\dfrac{9}{25}$ x $\dfrac{\square}{\square}$ = $\dfrac{\square}{100}$

$\dfrac{\square}{100}$ = ____ %

$\dfrac{9}{25}$ = ____ %

3 $\dfrac{3}{20}$ x $\dfrac{\square}{\square}$ = $\dfrac{\square}{100}$

$\dfrac{\square}{100}$ = ____ %

$\dfrac{3}{20}$ = ____ %

4 $\dfrac{1}{5}$ x $\dfrac{\square}{\square}$ = $\dfrac{\square}{100}$

$\dfrac{\square}{100}$ = ____ %

$\dfrac{1}{5}$ = ____ %

5 $\dfrac{7}{10}$ x $\dfrac{\square}{\square}$ = $\dfrac{\square}{100}$

$\dfrac{\square}{100}$ = ____ %

$\dfrac{7}{10}$ = ____ %

Write a ratio as a percent using a decimal.

6 $\dfrac{2}{5}$ → $5\overline{)2.00}$ with $.4$

$\dfrac{2}{5}$ = 0. ____

$\dfrac{2}{5}$ = ____ %

7 $\dfrac{1}{3}$ → $3\overline{)1.000}$ with $.3$

$\dfrac{1}{3}$ = 0. ____

$\dfrac{1}{3}$ = ____ %

8 $\dfrac{1}{2}$ → $2\overline{)1.00}$

$\dfrac{1}{2}$ = 0. ____

$\dfrac{1}{2}$ = ____ %

9 $\dfrac{3}{8}$ → $8\overline{)3.00}$

$\dfrac{3}{8}$ = 0. ____

$\dfrac{3}{8}$ = ____ %

10 $\dfrac{5}{6}$ → $6\overline{)5.00}$

$\dfrac{5}{6}$ = 0. ____

$\dfrac{5}{6}$ = ____ %

 Draw a circle around ratios that are repeating decimals.

●○○

Name _____

Find the percent of each number.

1 **Buy a sale item.**

25% of $40.00

$25\% = \dfrac{25}{100} = \dfrac{1}{4}$

$\dfrac{1}{4}$ x 40 = _____

25% of $40.00 = _____

Sale price is _____

Remember to simplify the ratio if you can.

Think:
$40 – _____

2 **Pay sales tax.**

6% of $54.00

6% = 0.06

0.06 x 54 = _____

6% of $54.00 = _____

Total cost is _____

Percent means parts per hundred. Write a decimal that shows hundredths.

Think:
$54 + _____

3 **Get a discount.**

10% of $250.00

10% = _____

_____ x _____ = _____

10% of $250.00 = _____

4 **Leave a tip.**

15% of $80.00

15% = _____

_____ x _____ = _____

15% of $80.00 = _____

5 8% of 125

8% = _____

_____ x _____ = _____

8% of 125 = _____

6 50% of 428

50% = _____

_____ x _____ = _____

50% of 428 = _____

7 $33\dfrac{1}{3}$% of $96

$33\dfrac{1}{3}$% = _____

_____ x _____ = _____

$33\dfrac{1}{3}$% of $96 = _____

8 45% of 540

45% = _____

_____ x _____ = _____

45% of 540 = _____

9 18% of $36.00

18% = _____

_____ x _____ = _____

18% of $36.00 = _____

10 20% of 100

20% = _____

_____ x _____ = _____

20% of 100 = _____

 Draw a circle around the problem that you can solve using mental math.

Find the percent of each number.

❶ 20% of 200

20% = $\frac{20}{100}$ = $\frac{1}{5}$

$\frac{1}{5}$ x 200 = _____

> When the percent is equivalent to the unit ratio, you can use mental math.

❷ 27% of 150

27% = 0.27

0.27 x 150 = _____

> It is easier to work with 27% as a decimal. You can use a calculator to multiply.

❸ 30% of 100   **❹** 14% of 150   **❺** 6% of 50   **❻** 15% of 150

_____   _____   _____   _____

❼ 10% of 145   **❽** 8% of 200   **❾** 50% of 532   **❿** 20% of 90

_____   _____   _____   _____

⓫ 20% of 48   **⓬** 55% of 30,000   **⓭** 40% of 85   **⓮** 200% of 300

_____   _____   _____   _____

Complete.

	SALE % OFF	Original Price	Amount Saved	Sale Price
⓯	25%	$56.00		
⓰	10%	$68.50		
⓱	40%	$75.00		
⓲	$33\frac{1}{3}$%	$200.00		
⓳	50%		$20.00	

 Tell why sometimes you write the percent as a fraction and other times as a decimal when you find the percent of a number.

Name _____

Find the percent of each number.

1 10% of 25　　**2** 75% of 100　　**3** 6% of 45　　**4** 25% of 200

_____　　　_____　　　_____　　　_____

5 15% of 100　　**6** 20% of 450　　**7** 30% of 19　　**8** 80% of 10

_____　　　_____　　　_____　　　_____

9 1% of 70　　**10** 10.5% of 300　　**11** 2% of 10,000　　**12** 16.5% of 6,000

_____　　　_____　　　_____　　　_____

13 $2\frac{1}{2}$% of 30　　**14** 85% of 600　　**15** 75% of 10　　**16** $10\frac{1}{4}$% of 50

_____　　　_____　　　_____　　　_____

Complete.

SALE % OFF	Original Price	Amount Saved	Sale Price
17 5%	$24.00		
18 20%		$11.30	
19 $33\frac{1}{3}$%	$90.00		
20 40%	$75.00		
21 10%		$30.00	

> Challenge! Think
> 10% x $\underline{n}$ = 30

 Write how you could find 15% of 40 using mental math.

Solve.

1 Luis left a 15% tip on a $30.00 food bill. How much did he leave for the tip?

2 Sue answered 80% of 150 test questions correctly. How many questions did she not answer correctly?

3 The dinner check was $58.00. If Fay gave the waiter a 20% tip, how much did she spend in all?

4 In a recent poll of 2,000 households, 29% had pets. How many households did not have pets?

5 The exam had 60 questions. Phelix got 85% correct. How many questions did he answer correctly?

6 The fabric costs $14.00 per yard. If you buy 5 yards or more, you can get 20% off. How much would five yards cost on sale?

Circle the letter for the correct answer.

7 Jay bought a cell phone that was originally sold for $126. It was on sale for $33\frac{1}{3}$% off the original price. How much did he pay for the phone?

a) $41.58

b) $42.00

c) $84.00

d) $93.00

8 The interest rate on the credit card is 15%. If we charge $200 to the credit card, how much will we pay including the interest?

a) $200

b) $215

c) $30

d) $230

Divide. Write the remainder as a whole number or as a fraction in simplest form.

❶

$$3\overline{)802} \quad \text{R} \underline{\quad}$$

Remember to write a zero in the quotient.

❷

$$7\overline{)4,560} \quad \dfrac{\square}{7}$$

❸

$$4\overline{)2300}$$

❹

$$5\overline{)8411} \quad \dfrac{\square}{5}$$

❺

$$8\overline{)2,432}$$

❻

$$10\overline{)3,197}$$

❼

$$12\overline{)692}$$

❽

$$16\overline{)13,604}$$

Divide. Write each remainder as a decir...

❾

$$4\overline{)425}$$

❿

$$8\overline{)538}$$

Remember to write a decimal point and zeros to continue dividing.

⓭ $512 \div 40$ **⓮** $391 \div 17$ **⓯** $903 \div 60$ **⓰** $444 \div 24$

 Look at the Problem 13. Tell how you can check your answer.

Name _____

Divide. Write each remainder as a whole number or as a fraction in simplest form.

1 $4\overline{)425}$ **2** $14\overline{)812}$ **3** $20\overline{)1,365}$ **4** $15\overline{)785}$

5 $512 \div 40$ **6** $282 \div 5$ **7** $6,984 \div 4$ **8** $5,428 \div 8$

Divide. Write each remainder as a whole decimal. Round to the nearest hundredth as necessary.

9 $8\overline{)250}$ **10** $16\overline{)1,526}$ **11** $4\overline{)765}$ **12** $48\overline{)954}$

13 $9,430 \div 20$ **14** $3,871 \div 7$ **15** $693 \div 10$ **16** $300 \div 16$

☆ **Show how you divide** $20\overline{)3,005}$ **. Label each step.**

Solve.

1 Sarah earned $114 in 8 hours. How much did she earn per hour?

2 Rafael's grandfather has 126 baseball cards in his collection. If the grandfather gives the same number of cards to Rafael and his two sisters, how many cards does each sibling get?

3 Mike's boat can carry 40 people across the river. Last month 2,504 people rode on Mike's boat. What is the least number of trips that Mike could have made across that river?

4 There are 60 floorboards in the living room. The floor is 14 feet wide. If each floorboard is the exact same width, how wide is each floorboard?

5 Jenna has 300 centimeters of string. She needs 27 centimeters to make a necklace. How many necklaces can she make?

6 The fence is 106 meters long. Each section of fence is 3 meters long. How many sections were needed to complete the fence?

Circle the letter for the correct answer.

7 Anna bought 120 feet of copper wire. She cut it into 16 pieces of the same length. How long is one piece of copper wire?

a) 8 ft

b) 7.8 ft

c) 7.55 ft

d) $7\frac{1}{2}$ ft

8 Oliver buys 258 lbs of rice for his restaurant. He buys 20 bags of rice. How many pounds does each bag hold?

a) 12.6 lbs

b) 12.9 lbs

c) 1.29 lbs

d) 129 lbs

Unit 7
Add and Subtract Decimals

Standard

The Number System
Compute fluently with multi-digit numbers and find common factors and multiples.
6.NS.3. Fluently add, subtract, multiply, and divide multi-digit decimals using the standard algorithm for each operation.

Model the Skill

◆ Draw the following problems on the board.

$$
\begin{array}{r}
1.768 \\
+\quad 0.834 \\
\hline
\end{array}
\qquad
\begin{array}{r}
1.768 \\
-\quad 0.834 \\
\hline
\end{array}
$$

◆ **Say**: *Today we are going to be adding and subtracting decimals. Look at the first problem. What is the sum? (2.602) Explain how you found the sum.*

◆ **Say**: *Now look at the second problem. What is the difference? (0.934) Explain how you found the difference.*

◆ **Say**: *Remember to always align the decimal points when you add or subtract. Also remember to always place the decimal point in your answer.*

◆ Assign students the appropriate practice pages to support their understanding of the skill.

Assess the Skill

Use the following problems to pre-/post-assess students' understanding of the skill.

$$
\begin{array}{r}
3.058 \\
+\quad 1.431 \\
\hline
\end{array}
\qquad
\begin{array}{r}
3.058 \\
-\quad 1.431 \\
\hline
\end{array}
\qquad
\begin{array}{r}
0.799 \\
+\quad 1.04 \\
\hline
\end{array}
\qquad
\begin{array}{r}
0.768 \\
-\quad 0.08 \\
\hline
\end{array}
$$

Name _____

Use models and place value. Find each sum or difference.

1 0.25 + 0.38 = _____

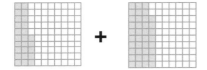

2 1.50 − 0.19 = _____

3 0.4 + 0.27 = _____

4 0.62 − 0.3 = _____

5

ones	.	tenths	hundredths
0	.	4	7
+ 1	.	6	8

6

ones	.	tenths	hundredths
2	.	3	
− 1	.	1	6

7

ones	.	tenths	hundredths	thousandths
2	.	7	1	5
+ 1	.	3	0	5

8

ones	.	tenths	hundredths	thousandths
5	.	2		
− 1	.	7	6	2

 Look at the page. Draw a circle around a model that shows five-tenths.

Name _____

Use place value. Find each sum or difference.

ones	.	tenths	hundredths	thousandths
	.			
+	.			

> Remember to place the decimal point in your answer.

❶
```
   1.07
+  0.89
_____
```

❷
```
   0.3
+  0.75
_____
```

❸
```
   2.265
+  0.834
_____
```

❹
```
   0.508
+  0.09
_____
```

❺
```
   5.25
-  0.79
_____
```

❻
```
   1.2
-  0.7
_____
```

❼
```
   1.8
-  1.671
_____
```

❽
```
   3.891
-  0.054
_____
```

❾ 2.09 + 1.37
_____

❿ 1.15 + 0.95
_____

⓫ 0.08 + 2.26
_____

⓬ 3.61 + 1.49
_____

> Remember to align the decimal points when you add or subtract.

⓭ 1.31 – 0.22
_____

⓮ 3.5 – 1.38
_____

⓯ 4.762 – 1.29
_____

⓰ 2.85 + 1.747
_____

☆ **Tell how you use place value to add decimals.**

Find each sum.

1

0.8 + 0.47 = _____

2

0.72 + 0.3 = _____

3

1.5 + 0.8 = _____

4

0.64 + 0.541 = _____

5
```
    1.56
 +  1.34
_____
```

6
```
    1.08
 +  2.66
_____
```

7
```
    1.405
 +  0.79
_____
```

8
```
    0.04
 +  1.39
_____
```

9
```
    1.17
 +  0.45
_____
```

10
```
    1.4
 +  0.67
_____
```

11
```
    1.53
 +  0.83
_____
```

12
```
    2.253
 +  0.595
_____
```

Find each difference.

13

0.5 – 0.34 = _____

14

0.76 – 0.6 = _____

15

1.4 – 0.07 = _____

16

2.28 – 1.31 = _____

17
```
    6.45
 -  0.62
_____
```

18
```
    2.04
 -  0.71
_____
```

19
```
    1.95
 -  0.99
_____
```

20
```
    0.7
 -  0.45
_____
```

21
```
    6.305
 -  0.15
_____
```

22
```
    4.28
 -  0.98
_____
```

23
```
    0.07
 -  0.005
_____
```

24
```
    2.375
 -  0.804
_____
```

 Look at the Problem 20. How do you know your answer is reasonable?

Solve.

1 Abby buys a jacket for $37.55 and a skirt for $18.95. What is the total amount she pays?

2 Brittany bought a dozen eggs for $3.98. Alex bought a dozen eggs for $2.49. How much more did Brittany pay for eggs?

3 Luke buys a small pizza for $7.99 and a large pizza with extra cheese for $14.25. How much did he spend on pizza altogether?

4 A small shampoo bottle contains 8.35 ounces. The large bottle of shampoo has 16.5 ounces. How much more shampoo do you get in the large bottle?

5 The concert tickets cost $32.50 each. This price includes a $4.75 service charge for each ticket. What is the face value of the concert ticket without the service charge?

6 The marathon is 26.2 miles long. Jen has run 22.7 miles so far. How many more miles does she have left before she crosses the finish line?

Circle the letter for the correct answer.

7 The temperature rose from 49.3°F to 65.8°F. How much did the temperature increase?

a) 115.1°F

b) 65.8°F

c) 49.3°F

d) 16.5°F

8 Okhee had fifty dollars. She spent $38.63 at the grocery store. Then she spent another $2.89 at the hardware store. How much money does she have left?

a) $35.74

b) $41.52

c) $8.48

d) $11.37

Unit 8
Multiply and Divide Decimals

Standard

The Number System
Compute fluently with multi-digit numbers and find common factors and multiples.
6.NS.3. Fluently add, subtract, multiply, and divide multi-digit decimals using the standard algorithm for each operation.

Model the Skill

◆ Write the following problems on the board.

$$0.6 \leftarrow 1 \text{ Decimal place}$$
$$\times \ 0.2 \leftarrow 1 \text{ Decimal place}$$
$$0.\square\square \leftarrow 2 \text{ Decimal places}$$

◆ **Say**: *Today we are going to be multiplying and dividing decimals. Look at the first problem. What is the product? (0.12) Remember that your answer must include the total number of decimal places for both factors, so you will have to fill the empty places with zeros as needed. Explain how you multiply decimals.*

$$3.6 \overline{)90} \qquad 36. \overline{)90.0} \qquad 36\overline{)90.0}$$

◆ **Say**: *Now look at the second problem. What is the quotient? (25) Remember to multiply the divisor by a power of 10 to make a whole number. Multiply the dividend by the same number. Explain how you divide.*

◆ Assign students the appropriate practice pages to support their understanding of the skill.

Assess the Skill

Use the following problems to pre-/post-assess students' understanding of the skill.

3.2 x 0.75	5.8 ÷ 0.02
0.4 x 1.8	1.62 ÷ 0.8
9.1 x 0.86	50.85 ÷ 0.625

Name _____

Find each product.

1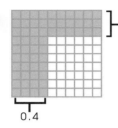
]—0.3

0.3 ← 1 Decimal place
x 0.4 ← 1 Decimal place
0.☐☐ ← 2 Decimal places

0.4

2   1.8 ← 1 Decimal place
x 0.7 ← 1 Decimal place
☐.☐☐

3   0.14 ← __ Decimal places
x 0.6 ← __ Decimal places
← __ Decimal places

Remember to write zeros in the product as needed.

4   1.26 ← __ Decimal places
x 0.32 ← __ Decimal places
☐☐☐
☐☐☐
← __ Decimal places

5 4.8 x 1 = _____

4.8 x 10 = _____

4.8 x 100 = _____

6 2.15 x 1 = _____

2.15 x 10 = _____

2.15 x 100 = _____

Find each quotient.

7 4.8)‾1‾2‾0‾ → 48.)‾1‾2‾0‾.‾0‾

4.8 x 10   12 x 10

Think: Multiply the divisor by a power of 10 to make a whole number. Multiply the dividend by the same number.

8 2.15)‾9‾.‾0‾3‾   215.)‾9‾0‾3‾.‾0‾0‾
x 100   x 100

9 3)‾1‾9‾.‾3‾5‾

Remember to place the decimal point in the quotient.

10 6.8 ÷ 0.32

Think: Multiply 0.32 by 100 and 6. 8 x 100. Then divide.

☆ **Look at your work. Draw a circle around the quotient that has 4 in the thousandths place.**

Solve.

1 Ava bought 3.5 kilograms of grapes for $8.68. How much does 1 kilogram of grapes cost?

2 Jordan has $10.00. If each drawing pen costs $1.49, how many can he buy?

3 Tyler's cat had 7 kittens. Each one weighed about 3.75 ounces. How much did they weigh altogether?

4 Marina bought 2.6 pounds of salmon at the fish market. The total cost was $38.87. What was the price of the salmon per pound?

5 The price of the jacket is $60. The sales tax is 8% of the price. How much is the sales tax on the jacket?

6 The dinner check was $78.00. If Erin leaves a 20% tip, how much will the tip be?

Circle the letter for the correct answer.

7 What is the product of 0.14 and 0.03?

a) 0.0042

b) 0.042

c) 0.42

d) 4.2

8 What is the quotient of 3.92 divided by 0.04?

a) 980

b) 98

c) 9.8

d) 0.98

Unit 9
Greatest Common Factor and Least Common Multiple

Standard

The Number System
Compute fluently with multi-digit numbers and find common factors and multiples.
6.NS.4. Find the greatest common factor of two whole numbers less than or equal to 100 and the least common multiple of two whole numbers less than or equal to 12. Use the distributive property to express a sum of two whole numbers 1–100 with a common factor as a multiple of a sum of two whole numbers with no common factor. For example, express 36 + 8 as 4 (9 + 2).

Model the Skill

- **Ask**: *What are the factors of 12?* (1, 2, 3, 4, 6, 12) *What are the factors of 8?* (1, 2, 4, 8) List the factors on the board.

- **Ask**: *What are the common factors of 12 and 8?* (1, 2, 4) *If the common factors are 1, 2, and 4, what is the greatest common factor of 12 and 8?* (4)

- **Ask**: *What are six multiples of 12?* (12, 24, 36, 48, 60, 72) *What are six multiples of 8?* (8, 16, 24, 32, 40, 48) List the multiples on the board.

- **Ask**: *What is the least common multiple of 12 and 8?* (24)

- Repeat with other number pairs. Then assign students the appropriate practice pages to support their understanding of the skill.

Assess the Skill

Use the following problems to pre-/post-assess students' understanding of the skill.

GCF of 5 and 10: _____

LCM of 5 and 10: _____

GCF of 6 and 9: _____

LCM of 6 and 9: _____

Name _____

Unit 9 • **Greatest Common Factor and Least Common Multiple**

List all the factors of each number.

1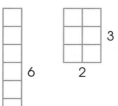

Factors of 6: ___ ___ ___ ___

2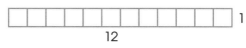

Factors of 12: ___ ___ ___ ___ ___ ___

3 What are the common factors of 6 and 12?

_____

4 What is the greatest common factor (GCF) of 6 and 12?

_____

5 Factors of 15: _____

Factors of 20: _____

6 What is the GCF of 15 and 20?

_____

Write the first 5 multiples of each number.

7

x	1	2	3	4	5
3	3	6	_	_	_

Multiples of 3: _____

8

x	1	2	3	4	5
5	5	10	_	_	_

Multiples of 5: _____

9 What is the least common multiple (LCM) of 3 and 5? _____

> Think: The least number other than 0 that is a multiple of each.

10 Multiples of 4: _____

Multiples of 6: _____

11 What is the LCM of 4 and 6?

_____

☆ **50 is a multiple of what number? Draw a circle around that number.**

Unit 9 • Common Core Mathematics Grade 6 • ©2012 Newmark Learning, LLC   47

List all the factors for each number. Circle the common factors.

1 Factors of 8: _____

Factors of 12: _____

Greatest common factor (GCF) of 8 and 12: _____

> Remember a factor of a number divides that number evenly.

2 Factors of 9: _____

Factors of 15: _____

GCF of 9 and 15: _____

3 Factors of 4: _____

Factors of 6: _____

GCF of 4 and 6: _____

4 Factors of 6: _____

Factors of 10: _____

Factors of 28: _____

GCF of 6, 10, and 28: _____

5 Factors of 12: _____

Factors of 15: _____

Factors of 18: _____

GCF of 12, 15, and 18: _____

Write the first 5 multiples of each number, other than 0. Circle the common multiples.

6 Multiples of 4: _____

Multiples of 5: _____

Least common multiple (LCM) of 4 and 5: _____

> Think:
> 4 x 1, 4 x 2, 4 x 3, 4 x 4, and 4 x 5

7 Multiples of 3: _____

Multiples of 10: _____

LCM of 3 and 10: _____

8 Multiples of 9: _____

Multiples of 15: _____

LCM of 9 and 15: _____

9 Multiples of 6: _____

Multiples of 9: _____

LCM of 6 and 9: _____

10 Multiples of 8: _____

Multiples of 12: _____

LCM of 8 and 12: _____

☆ **Tell how you can find the LCM of 4, 7, and 14.**

Name _____

Find the greatest common factor (GCF) of each set of numbers.

1 10 and 25

GCF_____

2 12 and 8

GCF_____

3 6 and 15

GCF_____

4 24 and 60

GCF_____

5 16 and 6

GCF_____

6 12 and 21

GCF_____

7 10 and 30

GCF_____

8 16, 18, and 30

GCF_____

9 20, 36, and 48

GCF_____

Find the least common multiple (LCM) other than 0 of each set of numbers.

10 7 and 9

LCM: _____

11 4 and 10

LCM: _____

12 3 and 5

LCM: _____

13 4 and 6

LCM: _____

14 9 and 6

LCM: _____

15 8 and 12

LCM: _____

16 8 and 3

LCM: _____

17 3 and 23

LCM: _____

18 14 and 6

LCM: _____

 Why do we not use 0 as the LCM of two numbers? Explain your thinking.

_____

_____

Solve.

1 Dan rides his bike to town every eighth day. Soo walks to town every third day. On which days are they likely to meet in town?

2 32/96 of the parents in the PTA wanted a bake sale instead of a car wash. What is the greatest common factor that you could use to simplify this fraction?

3 The ratio of students with bikes to students with scooters in the school is 85:51. What is the greatest common factor that you could use to simplify this ratio?

4 The biology class has a lab every 4 days. The earth science class has a lab every 3 days. On which day do both classes have lab?

5 What is the greatest common factor of 63 and 21?

6 What is the least common multiple of 7 and 12?

Circle the letter for the correct answer.

7 Twenty-eight girls and 35 boys signed up for the team challenge. Each team needs to have an equal number of girls and boys. What is the greatest number of teams possible?

a) 31

b) 14

c) 7

d) 5

8 Every 10 years the alumni have a reunion. Every 2 years the alumni have a soccer game. How often do the reunion and the game fall in the same year?

a) Once every 10 years

b) 5 times every 10 years

c) 20 times every 10 years

d) None of the above

Unit 10
Multiply Fractions

Standard

The Number System
Apply and extend previous understandings of multiplication and division to divide fractions by fractions.
6.NS.1. Interpret and compute quotients of fractions, and solve word problems involving division of fractions by fractions.

Model the Skill

◆ Draw the following problem on the board.

$$\frac{1}{3} \times \frac{3}{4} = \underline{\quad}$$

◆ **Say**: *Today we are going to be multiplying fractions. Look at the problem. What is the product?* (3/12 or 1/4) *Explain how you multiplied.* Remind students to find a common factor of any numerator and denominator and then simplify.

◆ Then practice multiplying whole numbers by converting whole numbers to improper fractions. **Ask**: *What is the product of 6 and 2/3?* (4)

$$6 \times \frac{2}{3} = \underline{\quad} \qquad \frac{6}{1} \times \frac{2}{3} = \underline{\quad}$$

◆ Assign students the appropriate practice page(s) to support their understanding of the skill.

Assess the Skill

Use the following problems to pre-/post-assess students' understanding of the skill.

$$\frac{1}{4} \times \frac{3}{4} = \underline{\quad} \qquad \frac{1}{2} \times \frac{4}{5} = \underline{\quad} \qquad \frac{2}{3} \times \frac{2}{3} = \underline{\quad}$$

$$4 \times \frac{1}{2} = \underline{\quad} \qquad \frac{5}{8} \times \frac{2}{5} = \underline{\quad} \qquad \frac{6}{7} \times \frac{1}{10} = \underline{\quad}$$

Name _____

Multiply. Write the answer in simplest form.

1 $\dfrac{1}{2}$ of $\dfrac{3}{4}$

$\dfrac{1}{2}$ × $\dfrac{3}{4}$ = _____

2 $\dfrac{1}{2}$ of $\dfrac{1}{4}$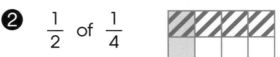

$\dfrac{1}{2}$ × $\dfrac{1}{4}$ = _____

3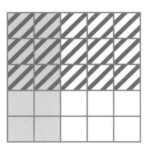

$\dfrac{2}{5}$ × $\dfrac{3}{5}$ = _____

4 $\dfrac{7}{8}$ × $\dfrac{1}{7}$ = _____

$\div 7$

$\dfrac{7}{8}$ × $\dfrac{1}{7}$ = _____

$\div 7$

$\dfrac{1}{8}$ × $\dfrac{1}{1}$ = _____

> Remember to find a common factor of any numerator and denominator then simplify.

5 $\dfrac{1}{3}$ × 6 = _____

> Remember to write the whole number as a fraction then multiply.

$\dfrac{1}{3}$ × $\dfrac{6}{1}$ = _____

6 $\dfrac{3}{8}$ × 16 = _____

$\div 8$

$\dfrac{3}{8}$ × $\dfrac{16}{1}$ = _____

$\div 8$

> Remember to simplify.

$\dfrac{3}{1}$ × $\dfrac{2}{1}$ = _____

7 $\dfrac{2}{5}$ × $2\dfrac{1}{4}$

> Remember to write the mixed number as an improper fraction then multiply.

$\dfrac{2}{5}$ × $\dfrac{9}{4}$

_____

8 $1\dfrac{2}{3}$ of $2\dfrac{1}{2}$

 $\dfrac{\square}{3}$ × $\dfrac{\square}{2}$

_____

 Look at the page. Draw a circle around fractions you can simplify before multiplying.

●○○

Name _____

Multiply. Write the answer in simplest form.

1 $\frac{1}{3}$ of $\frac{1}{2}$

$\frac{1}{3}$ × $\frac{1}{2}$ = _____

2 $\frac{1}{8}$ of $\frac{4}{5}$ = _____

$\frac{1}{8}$ × $\frac{4}{5}$ = _____ ÷4 ÷4

$\frac{1}{2}$ × $\frac{1}{5}$ = _____

> Remember to simplify first, when possible. Divide any numerator and denominator by a common factor.

3 $\frac{1}{3}$ × $\frac{3}{4}$ = _____

4 $\frac{3}{6}$ × $\frac{3}{4}$ = _____

5 $\frac{5}{8}$ × $\frac{6}{10}$ = _____

> Think: Write the whole number as a fraction.

6 $\frac{1}{4}$ of 12

$\frac{1}{4}$ × $\frac{12}{1}$ = _____

7 $\frac{3}{5}$ of 10

$\frac{3}{5}$ × $\frac{10}{1}$ = _____

8 $\frac{5}{6}$ of 9

$\frac{5}{6}$ × $\frac{9}{1}$ = _____

9 $\frac{2}{3}$ of 14

$\frac{2}{3}$ × $\frac{14}{1}$ = _____

10 $\frac{3}{4}$ of 16

$\frac{3}{4}$ × $\frac{16}{1}$ = _____

11 $\frac{1}{8}$ of 24

$\frac{1}{8}$ × $\frac{24}{1}$ = _____

12 $\frac{3}{8}$ × $4\frac{1}{2}$

$\frac{3}{8}$ × $\frac{9}{2}$

> Think: Write the mixed number as an improper fraction.

13 $\frac{1}{6}$ × $4\frac{1}{5}$

$\frac{1}{6}$ × $\frac{21}{5}$

14 $\frac{5}{8}$ × $2\frac{2}{3}$

$\frac{5}{8}$ × $\frac{8}{3}$

15 $\frac{4}{9}$ × $3\frac{1}{3}$

$\frac{4}{9}$ × $\frac{10}{3}$

16 $\frac{3}{5}$ × $7\frac{1}{2}$

$\frac{3}{5}$ × $\frac{15}{2}$

17 3 × $5\frac{1}{6}$

3 × $\frac{31}{6}$

 Tell how you found the product for Problem 5.

Name _____

Multiply. Write the answer in simplest form.

❶ $\dfrac{2}{3}$ x $\dfrac{3}{5}$ 　　**❷** $\dfrac{2}{7}$ x $\dfrac{1}{4}$ 　　**❸** $\dfrac{3}{8}$ x $\dfrac{1}{3}$ 　　**❹** $\dfrac{4}{5}$ x $\dfrac{3}{4}$

_____　　_____　　_____　　_____

❺ $\dfrac{3}{8}$ x 4 　　**❻** $\dfrac{2}{3}$ x 6 　　**❼** $\dfrac{1}{5}$ x 7 　　**❽** $\dfrac{3}{4}$ x 2

_____　　_____　　_____　　_____

❾ $1\dfrac{1}{4}$ x 2 　　**❿** $3\dfrac{1}{6}$ x 4 　　**⓫** $1\dfrac{2}{3}$ x 6 　　**⓬** $4\dfrac{3}{4}$ x 5

_____　　_____　　_____　　_____

⓭ $\dfrac{2}{3}$ x $\dfrac{7}{8}$ 　　**⓮** $\dfrac{3}{9}$ x 12 　　**⓯** $6\dfrac{1}{4}$ x 2 　　**⓰** $\dfrac{5}{8}$ x 6

_____　　_____　　_____　　_____

⓱ $\dfrac{2}{7}$ x $\dfrac{4}{8}$ 　　**⓲** $\dfrac{3}{10}$ x 5 　　**⓳** $6\dfrac{1}{3}$ x 10 　　**⓴** $\dfrac{6}{8}$ x 7

_____　　_____　　_____　　_____

☆ **Write how you solved Problem 9. Draw a picture to prove your answer is correct.**

_____

_____

Solve.

1 Andy carried $\frac{1}{2}$ gallon of water on a hike. He drank $\frac{2}{3}$ of the water. How much water did he drink?

2 Felice bought $\frac{3}{4}$ of a pound of American cheese at the deli. She used $\frac{1}{2}$ of the cheese to make sandwiches. How much cheese did she use?

3 Jesse has 5 and $\frac{3}{4}$ dozen eggs. How many eggs does Jesse have?

4 Pierre is running 26 and $\frac{2}{10}$ miles in the marathon. He has run $\frac{3}{4}$ of the way. How far has he run?

5 Slater's room is 5 meters long and $3\frac{1}{4}$ meters wide. What is the area of Slater's room?

6 Gloria has $2\frac{5}{8}$ ounces of perfume. If she uses one third of it, how much will she have left?

Circle the letter for the correct answer.

7 Olivia has $1\frac{1}{5}$ yards of fabric. She uses $\frac{5}{8}$ of the fabric to make a shirt. How much fabric did she use?

a) $\frac{1}{8}$ yard

b) $\frac{2}{4}$ yard

c) $\frac{3}{4}$ yard

d) $\frac{1}{5}$ yard

8 We have $4\frac{3}{4}$ pounds of apples in each bag. If we have 4 bags, how many pounds of apples do we have in all?

a) $\frac{1}{4}$ pound

b) $1\frac{1}{4}$ pounds

c) $18\frac{3}{4}$ pounds

d) 19 pounds

Unit 11
Divide Fractions

Standard

The Number System
Apply and extend previous understandings of multiplication and division to divide fractions by fractions.
6.NS.1. Interpret and compute quotients of fractions, and solve word problems involving division of fractions by fractions.

Model the Skill

◆ Draw the following problem on the board.

$$\frac{1}{2} \div \frac{1}{4} = \underline{\hspace{2cm}} \qquad\qquad \frac{1}{2} \div \frac{1}{4} = \frac{1}{2} \times \frac{4}{1}$$

◆ **Say**: *Today we are going to be dividing fractions. Look at the problem. What is the quotient? Explain how you divide fractions.* (First find the reciprocal, then multiply by the reciprocal).

◆ **Ask**: *How do you divide whole numbers by fractions.* (First convert the whole number to an improper fraction, then find the reciprocal, and multiply).

◆ **Ask**: *What is the quotient of 6 divided by 3/5?* (10)

$$6 \div \frac{3}{5} = \underline{\hspace{2cm}} \qquad\qquad \frac{6}{1} \div \frac{3}{5} = \frac{6}{1} \times \frac{5}{3}$$

◆ Assign students the appropriate practice pages to support their understanding of the skill.

Assess the Skill

Use the following problems to pre-/post-assess students' understanding of the skill.

$$\frac{1}{4} \div \frac{3}{4} = \underline{\hspace{1.5cm}} \qquad \frac{1}{2} \div \frac{4}{5} = \underline{\hspace{1.5cm}} \qquad \frac{2}{3} \div \frac{2}{3} = \underline{\hspace{1.5cm}}$$

$$4 \div \frac{1}{2} = \underline{\hspace{1.5cm}} \qquad \frac{5}{8} \div \frac{2}{5} = \underline{\hspace{1.5cm}} \qquad \frac{6}{7} \div \frac{1}{10} = \underline{\hspace{1.5cm}}$$

Name _____

Find each reciprocal.

❶ $\dfrac{1}{4} \times r = 1$

$\dfrac{1}{4} \times \dfrac{\Box}{1} = 1$

$r = $ _____

❷ $\dfrac{2}{3} \times r = 1$

$\dfrac{2}{3} \times \dfrac{\Box}{2} = 1$

$r = $ _____

❸ $r \times \dfrac{2}{1} = 1$

$\dfrac{1}{2} \times \dfrac{\Box}{1} = 1$

$r = $ _____

❹ $\dfrac{3}{8} \times r = 1$

$\dfrac{3}{8} \times \dfrac{\Box}{3} = 1$

$r = $ _____

Divide. Write the answer in simplest form.

❺ How many $\dfrac{1}{2}$'s are in 4?

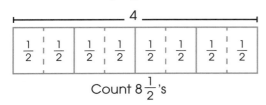

Count $8\frac{1}{2}$'s

$4 \div \dfrac{1}{2} = 4 \times \dfrac{2}{1}$

$4 \times \dfrac{2}{1} = $ _____

so $4 \div \dfrac{1}{2} = $ _____

Think: $\dfrac{2}{1}$ is the reciprocal of $\dfrac{1}{2}$. Multiply by the reciprocal.

❻ How many $\dfrac{2}{3}$'s are in 4?

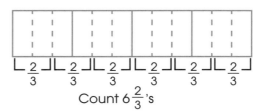

Count $6\frac{2}{3}$'s

$4 \div \dfrac{2}{3} = 4 \times \dfrac{3}{2}$

$4 \times \dfrac{3}{2} = $ _____

so $4 \div \dfrac{2}{3} = $ _____

❼ $\dfrac{3}{4} \div \dfrac{1}{8}$

$\dfrac{3}{4} \div \dfrac{1}{8} = \dfrac{3}{4} \times \dfrac{\Box}{1}$

$\dfrac{3}{4} \times \dfrac{\Box}{1} = $ _____

so $\dfrac{3}{4} \div \dfrac{1}{8} = $ _____

Remember to multiply by the reciprocal.

❽ $\dfrac{2}{3} \div \dfrac{3}{4}$

$\dfrac{2}{3} \div \dfrac{3}{4} = \dfrac{2}{3} \times \dfrac{\Box}{3}$

$\dfrac{2}{3} \times \dfrac{\Box}{3} = $ _____

so $\dfrac{2}{3} \div \dfrac{3}{4} = $ _____

Think: Check your answer.

$\dfrac{\Box}{\Box} \times \dfrac{3}{4} = \dfrac{2}{3}$

 Draw a circle around the reciprocal of $\dfrac{3}{4}$. Tell why it is a reciprocal.

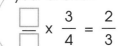

Name _____

Divide. Write the answer in simplest form.

1 How many $\frac{1}{4}$'s are in 3?

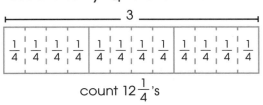

count 12 $\frac{1}{4}$'s

$3 \div \frac{1}{4} = 3 \times \frac{4}{1}$

$3 \times \frac{4}{1} =$ _____

so $3 \div \frac{1}{4} =$ _____

Remember $\frac{4}{1}$ is the reciprocal of $\frac{1}{4}$. Multiply by the reciprocal.

2 How many $\frac{1}{4}$'s are in $\frac{5}{8}$?

$\frac{5}{8} \div \frac{1}{4} = \frac{5}{8} \times \frac{\square}{\square}$

$\frac{5}{8} \times \frac{\square}{\square} =$ _____

so $\frac{5}{8} \div \frac{1}{4} =$ _____

Remember, you can simplify fractions *before* you multiply.

3 $6 \div \frac{3}{5} =$ ____

4 $3 \div \frac{5}{8} =$ ____

5 $7 \div \frac{2}{3} =$ ____

6 $10 \div \frac{7}{9} =$ ____

7 $\frac{3}{8} \div \frac{2}{6} =$ ____

8 $\frac{5}{6} \div \frac{1}{9} =$ ____

9 $\frac{2}{3} \div \frac{1}{9} =$ ____

10 $\frac{5}{9} \div \frac{1}{10} =$ ____

11 $\frac{5}{6} \div \frac{3}{4} =$ ____

12 $\frac{9}{10} \div \frac{1}{8} =$ ____

13 $12 \div \frac{2}{5} =$ ____

14 $6 \div \frac{3}{8} =$ ____

15 $\frac{7}{8} \div \frac{4}{5} =$ ____

16 $\frac{1}{4} \div 8 =$ ____

17 $\frac{6}{5} \div \frac{1}{5} =$ ____

18 $\frac{3}{5} \div \frac{1}{12} =$ ____

 Tell how you can check your answer for Problem 3.

Divide. Write the answer in simplest form.

1 $4 \div \dfrac{3}{5} =$ _____

2 $6 \div \dfrac{2}{3} =$ _____

3 $10 \div \dfrac{4}{5} =$ _____

4 $3 \div \dfrac{7}{8} =$ _____

5 $2 \div \dfrac{5}{6} =$ _____

6 $9 \div \dfrac{1}{8} =$ _____

7 $5 \div \dfrac{2}{3} =$ _____

8 $14 \div \dfrac{7}{8} =$ _____

9 $\dfrac{1}{5} \div \dfrac{1}{4} =$ _____

10 $\dfrac{1}{3} \div \dfrac{3}{8} =$ _____

11 $\dfrac{9}{10} \div \dfrac{2}{5} =$ _____

12 $\dfrac{3}{4} \div \dfrac{1}{6} =$ _____

13 $\dfrac{3}{5} \div \dfrac{2}{3} =$ _____

14 $\dfrac{4}{7} \div \dfrac{1}{6} =$ _____

15 $\dfrac{1}{10} \div \dfrac{1}{8} =$ _____

16 $\dfrac{5}{12} \div \dfrac{5}{6} =$ _____

17 $2\dfrac{1}{4} \div \dfrac{1}{4} =$ _____

18 $3\dfrac{2}{5} \div \dfrac{7}{10} =$ _____

19 $1\dfrac{2}{3} \div \dfrac{5}{6} =$ _____

20 $4\dfrac{2}{3} \div \dfrac{2}{3} =$ _____

21 $5\dfrac{1}{5} \div \dfrac{8}{9} =$ _____

22 $2\dfrac{3}{8} \div \dfrac{3}{4} =$ _____

23 $6\dfrac{1}{2} \div \dfrac{3}{4} =$ _____

24 $2\dfrac{6}{7} \div \dfrac{3}{10} =$ _____

 Write the steps you take to divide a fraction by a fraction. Use an example from one of the problems above.

Solve.

1 Ardit has 8 chapters of a book left to read. He reads $\frac{2}{3}$ of a chapter each day. How many days does it take to finish reading the book?

2 Cameron cooks $\frac{3}{4}$ lb of pasta. If she serves the pasta in three even-size bowls, about how much does she put in each bowl?

3 Altogether, Renee walks a combined $2\frac{4}{5}$ miles to and from the train each day. How long is the walk to the train?

4 We have 10 gallons of gas in the car. We use $1\frac{5}{8}$ gallons each hour. How many hours of gas do we have?

5 Luisa ran $3\frac{2}{3}$ kilometers in $\frac{1}{3}$ of an hour. If speed is distance over time, calculate Luisa's speed.

6 Lin has 8 green apples and 2 red apples. If he slices the green apples in eighths, how many apple slices will he have?

Circle the letter for the correct answer.

7 Irma has $\frac{5}{6}$ yard of ribbon. She cuts it into $\frac{1}{6}$-yard pieces. How many pieces of ribbon does she have?

a) $\frac{5}{36}$

b) $\frac{5}{6}$

c) 5

d) 6

8 The area of the desk is $1\frac{4}{5}$ square meters. The length of the desk is 2 meters. What is the width of the desk?

a) $\frac{1}{8}$

b) $1\frac{1}{8}$

c) $\frac{9}{10}$

d) $3\frac{3}{5}$

Unit 12
Understand Integers

Standard

The Number System
Apply and extend previous understandings of numbers to the system of rational numbers.
6.NS.5. Understand that positive and negative numbers are used together to describe quantities having opposite directions or values (e.g., temperature above/below zero, elevation above/below sea level, credits/debits, positive/negative electric charge); use positive and negative numbers to represent quantities in real-world contexts, explaining the meaning of 0 in each situation.
6.NS.7. Understand ordering and absolute value of rational numbers.

Model the Skill

◆ Draw the following number line on the board.

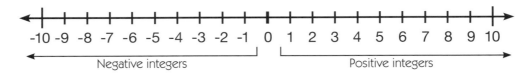

◆ **Say**: *Today we are going to be working with positive and negative integers. Which point on the number line represents negative 6? How do you know? Which point on the number line represents positive 3? How do you know?*

◆ **Say**: *The opposite of an integer is its positive or negative counterpart on the opposite side of the number line. So, whatever lies the exact distance from zero on the other side of the number line is an integer's opposite. The absolute value of an integer is the distance of a number on the number line from 0, no matter which direction from zero the number lies. The absolute value of a number is never negative.*

◆ **Ask**: *What is the opposite of positive 8?* (negative 8) *What is the absolute value of negative 8?* (8)

◆ Assign students the appropriate practice pages to support their understanding of the skill.

Assess the Skill

Use the following problems to pre-/post-assess students' understanding of the skill.

integer: _____   integer: –5   integer: 1

opposite: +9   opposite: _____   opposite: _____

absolute value: _____   absolute value: _____   absolute value: _____

Name _____

Write an integer to describe each situation.

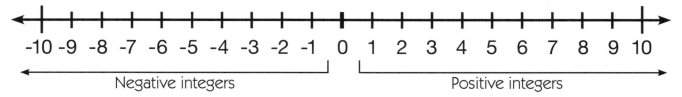

-10 -9 -8 -7 -6 -5 -4 -3 -2 -1   0   1   2   3   4   5   6   7   8   9   10

Negative integers   Positive integers

1 5 degrees above 0 _____

  3 degrees below 0 _____

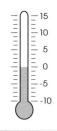

2 4 meters below sea level _____

  4 meters above sea level _____

3 A positive charge of 5 _____

  A negative charge of 7 _____

4 A savings of $100 _____

  A debt of $30 _____

Write the opposite of each integer. Then write the absolute value. Use the number line at the top of the page to help you.

5 integer: +2

  opposite: _____

  absolute value: |2|

Think: An integer is an equal distance from 0, but on the opposite side of 0.

6 integer: –3

  opposite: _____

  absolute value: _____

Think: Absolute value is a number's distance from 0 on the number line.

7 integer: 8

  opposite: _____

  absolute value: _____

8 integer: –5

  opposite: _____

  absolute value: _____

9 integer: 1

  opposite: _____

  absolute value: _____

☆ **Use the number line at the top of the page. Draw a circle around an integer with the absolute value of |7|.**

Write an integer to describe each situation. Draw a picture to show each.

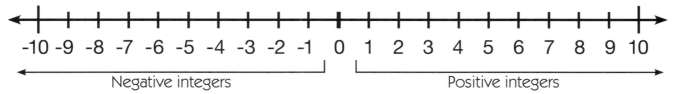

-10 -9 -8 -7 -6 -5 -4 -3 -2 -1 0 1 2 3 4 5 6 7 8 9 10

Negative integers   Positive integers

1 4 stories below ground level

_____

2 7 stories above ground level

_____

3 A temperature 20°C above freezing

_____

4 A temperature 5°C below freezing

_____

5 A withdrawal of $75.00

_____

6 A deposit of $150.00

_____

Complete. Use the number line at the top of the page to help you.

7 integer: –4

opposite: _____

absolute value: |4|

8 integer: –3

opposite: _____

absolute value: _____

9 integer: _____

opposite: +2

absolute value: _____

10 integer: –5

opposite: _____

absolute value: _____

11 integer: 1

opposite: _____

absolute value: _____

12 integer: _____

opposite: –16

absolute value: _____

13 integer: 107

opposite: _____

absolute value: _____

14 integer: –90

opposite: _____

absolute value: _____

 Tell how you find the absolute value of –3.

Name _____

Write an integer to describe each situation.

1 A deposit of fifty dollars
_____

2 A withdrawal of twenty dollars
_____

3 A decrease in profits of $300
_____

4 Sixteen degrees below zero
_____

5 1,200 meters above sea level
_____

6 A increase in profits of $500
_____

56 meters below sea level
_____

A positive charge of 6
_____

Complete.

7 integer: _____
opposite: +9
absolute value: _____

8 integer: +8
opposite: _____
absolute value: _____

9 integer: –94
opposite: _____
absolute value: _____

10 integer: _____
opposite: –2
absolute value: _____

11 integer: –15
opposite: _____
absolute value: _____

12 integer: +72
opposite: _____
absolute value: _____

13 integer: _____
opposite: +200
absolute value: _____

14 integer: +60
opposite: _____
absolute value: _____

15 integer: +19
opposite: _____
absolute value: _____

☆ **What are negative integers? Explain.**

Solve.

1 What integer would represent "ten degrees below zero"?

2 What integer would represent "twenty-two hundred feet above sea level"?

3 What is the opposite of 8?

4 What is the opposite of –45?

5 What is the absolute value of –12?

6 What is the absolute value of –674?

Circle the letter for the correct answer.

7 Which of the following is not an integer?

   a) 5

   b) 0

   c) 0.2

   d) –2

8 Which integer has an opposite of 9?

   a) 0.9

   b) 90

   c) –9

   d) 1/9

Unit 13
Order Rational Numbers on a Number Line

Standard

The Number System
Apply and extend previous understandings of numbers to the system of rational numbers.
6.NS.6. Understand a rational number as a point on the number line. Extend number line diagrams and coordinate axes familiar from previous grades to represent points on the line and in the plane with negative number coordinates.
6.NS.7. Understand ordering and absolute value of rational numbers.

Model the Skill

◆ Draw the following number line and problems on the board.

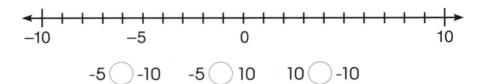

```
-5 ◯ -10    -5 ◯ 10    10 ◯ -10
```

◆ **Say**: *Today we are going to be comparing and ordering integers. Look at the number line. Use the number line to tell which number in each expression is greater. Then place the numbers in order. (-10 < -5 < 10)*

◆ **Say**: *Now plot the following points on the number line: -8, 7, -3, 6, 2, -1*

◆ Assign students the appropriate practice pages to support their understanding of the skill.

Assess the Skill

Use the following problems to pre-/post-assess students' understanding of the skill.

◆ Ask students to use > or < to make each statement true.

```
-4 ◯ -18    -12 ◯ 6    3 ◯ -3
```

◆ Ask students to plot the following points on the number line: -6, 3, 8, -5, -4

```
←——+——+——+——+——+——+——+——+——+——+——+——+——+——+——+——+——+——+——+——+——→
  -10                          0                          10
```

Name _____

Solve. Then place the integer on the number line.

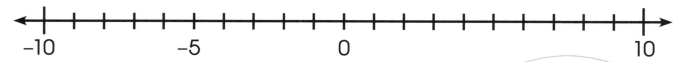

1 An integer whose opposite is –5 _____

> Remember: An opposite integer is an equal distance from 0, but on the opposite side of 0.

2 Two integers whose absolute value is 131 _____

> Think: Absolute value is a number's distance from 0 on the number line.

3 An integer whose opposite is 2 _____

4 Two integers whose absolute value is 191 _____

5 An integer greater than –8 and less than –6 _____

> Think: Numbers to the right on a number line are greater. What integer is to the right of –8?

Complete the number line above. Write > or < to make each statement true.

6 –2 ◯ –3

> Think: –2 is to the right of –3 on the number line.

7 –6 ◯ 1

> Think: Where is –6 on the number line? Is it to the right or left of 1?

8 10 ◯ –10   **9** –5 ◯ –6   **10** 5 ◯ 6

11 –3 ◯ 2   **12** 4 ◯ –7   **13** 8 ◯ 7

14 –2 ◯ –7   **15** –9 ◯ 8   **16** 6 ◯ –6

 Use the number line at the top of the page. Place the number $\frac{1}{2}$ on it.

Solve. Then write the integer on the number line.

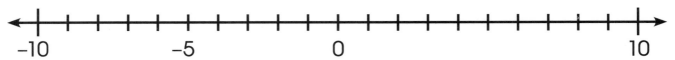

-10   -5   0   10

❶ An integer whose opposite is 1 _____

> Remember: An opposite integer is an equal distance from 0, but on the opposite side of 0.

❷ An integer whose opposite is 8 _____

❸ Two integers whose absolute value is 151 _____

> Think: Absolute value is a number's distance from 0 on the number line.

❹ Two integers whose absolute value is 27 _____

Complete the number line above. Write > or < to make each statement true.

❺ -9 ◯ -7   ❻ -2 ◯ -5   ❼ -6 ◯ -11   ❽ -4 ◯ -14

> Remember: Numbers to the right on a number line are greater.

❾ -12 ◯ -8   ❿ -7 ◯ -8   ⓫ -13 ◯ -19   ⓬ -16 ◯ -6

⓭ -5 ◯ -1   ⓮ -3 ◯ -10   ⓯ -6 ◯ 7   ⓰ -4 ◯ -8

⓱ -23 ◯ -25   ⓲ -73 ◯ -15   ⓳ -18 ◯ -81   ⓴ -2 ◯ 5

☆ **Fractions and decimals are also rational numbers. Tell where you would place $\frac{1}{2}$ and 3.5 on the number line.**

Solve. Then write the integer on the number line.

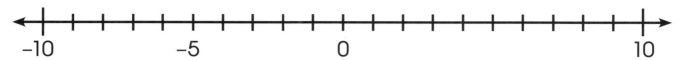

1 An integer whose opposite is 7
_____

2 Two integers whose absolute
value is 84 _____

3 An integer whose opposite is 16
_____

4 Two integers whose absolute
value is 252 _____

5 An integer whose opposite is –58
_____

6 An integer greater than –10 and
less than –8 _____

7 Two integers whose absolute
value is 14 _____

8 An integer greater than 7 and
less than 9 _____

Complete the number line above. Write > or < to make each statement true.

9 –12 ◯ –5

10 –4 ◯ –5

11 –18 ◯ 17

12 –6 ◯ –21

13 –7 ◯ –4

14 –18 ◯ –7

15 –3 ◯ 3

16 –19 ◯ –2

17 23 ◯ –8

18 –13 ◯ –15

19 –41 ◯ –51

20 –17 ◯ –71

21 –10 ◯ –25

22 –23 ◯ –9

23 –6 ◯ 5

24 –3 ◯ –19

☆ **Write how you solved the ninth problem. Draw a picture to prove your answer is correct.**

_____

_____

Name _____

Solve.

1 Which point on the number line is located at –4?

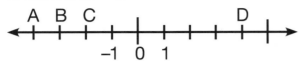

2 Write the integers 4, –7, 5, –2 in order from least to greatest.

3 Which point on the number line is located at 2?

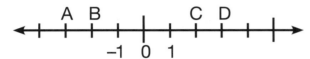

4 Write the integers 12, –14, 10, –20 in order from greatest to least.

5 Which point on the number line is located at –30?

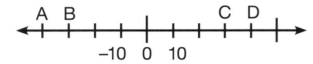

6 Write the integers –143, 125, –118, 60, –36 in order from least to greatest.

Circle the letter for the correct answer.

7 Which statement is true?

    a) –15 > –13

    b) 12 > –14

    c) 10 > 11

    d) –11 < –12

8 Which statement is false?

    a) –6 < –12

    b) –11 < 1

    c) 21 < 22

    d) –15 < –7

Unit 14
Graph Points on the Coordinate Plane

Standard

The Number System
Apply and extend previous understandings of numbers to the system of rational numbers.
6.NS.6. Understand a rational number as a point on the number line. Extend number line diagrams and coordinate axes familiar from previous grades to represent points on the line and in the plane with negative number coordinates.
6.NS.8. Solve real-world and mathematical problems by graphing points in all four quadrants of the coordinate plane. Include use of coordinates and absolute value to find distances between points with the same first coordinate or the same second coordinate.

Model the Skill

◆ Draw the coordinate plane on the board and label each quadrant.

◆ **Say**: *Today we are going to be graphing points on the coordinate plane. The coordinate plane has four sections, or quadrants. When we graph a point, we use coordinates to tell us the location of the point on the plane. We read the coordinates as (x, y), so the first value (x) tells us the point's place along the x axis, or horizontal axis. The second value (y) tells us the point's location along the y axis, or vertical axis.*

◆ Assist students in plotting and labeling the points A–D using the listed coordinates.

◆ Assign students the appropriate practice pages to support their understanding of the skill.

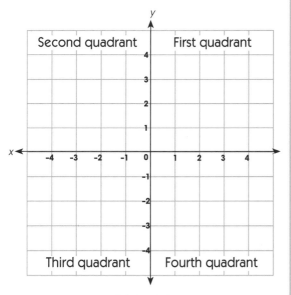

Point A (2, 1)
Point B (–2, 1)
Point C (–2, –1)
Point D (2, –1)

Assess the Skill

Use the following problems to pre-/post-assess students' understanding of the skill.

◆ Ask students to plot and label the points using the listed coordinates.

Point A (–3, 4)   Point R (0, 3)
Point B (2, –2)   Point S (–1, –3)
Point C (1, –4)   Point T (–2, 2)
Point D (–2, –3)   Point U (3, –4)

Plot each point using the given coordinates.

1 Point A (2, 3)

Think: Both coordinates are positive, so point A will be in the first quadrant.

2 Point B (3, 2)

3 Point C (−2, −3)

Think: both coordinates are negative, so point C will be in the third quadrant.

4 Point D (−3, −2)

5 Point E (2, −3)

Think: Move from 0 across to 2 and then down to −3.

6 Point F (3, −2)

7 Point G (−3, 2)

8 Point H (−2, 3)

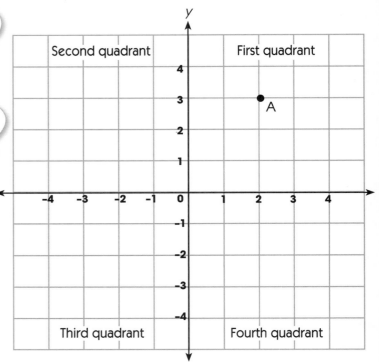

Plot each point using the given coordinates.

9

cups of flour (x)	2	4	6	8
cups of water (y)	1	2	3	4

Think: Move from 0 across x-axis to 2. Then move up to 1.

10

x	y
−6	4
−4	2
−2	0
0	−2
2	−4
4	−6

Think: Move from 0 across x-axis to −6. Then move up to 4.

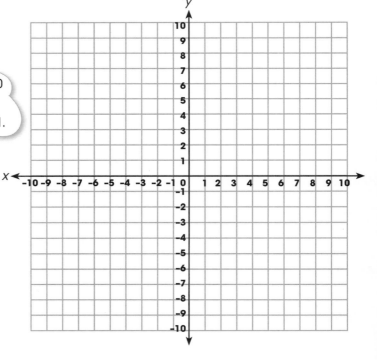

☆ **Look at Problem 9. Extend the line you graphed. How many cups of flour do you need for 5 cups of water?**

Plot each point using the given coordinate.

1 Point A (4, 1)

2 Point B (1, 4)

3 Point C (–2, –3)

4 Point D (–3, –2)

5 Point E (–4, 2)

6 Point F (3, –2)

7 Point G (–3, 2)

8 Point H (–2, 3)

Remember: The first coordinate in the pair represents x. Start at origin 0 and move across the x-axis to 4. Then move up to 1 and place the point.

Think: Move from 0 across to 2 and then down to –3.

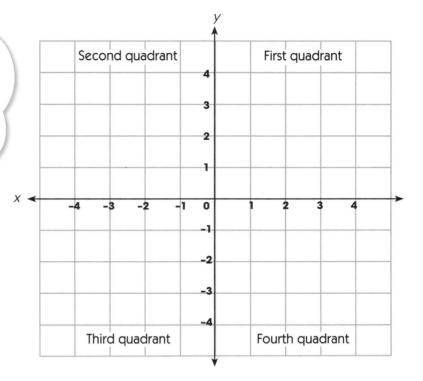

Graph the ordered pairs in each table. Then connect the points with a line.

9

x	y
–4	8
–3	6
–2	4
–1	2

10

x	y
5	–6
4	–5
3	–4
2	–3

Think: The coordinates are (–, +) so the points will be in the second quadrant.

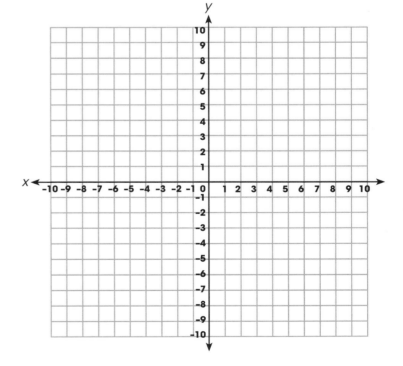

11

hours (x)	1	2	3	4
dollars (y)	2	4	6	8

☆ **Tell how you know just by looking at an ordered pair which quadrant on the plane it will fall in.**

Name _____

Write the coordinate or plot each point.

1 Point A (__, __)

> Remember, x is the first number, y is the second number.

2 Point B (__, __)

3 Point C (__, __)

4 Point D (__, __)

5 Point E (–5, –2)

6 Point F (–2, –1)

7 Point G (4, –2)

8 Point H (–2, –3)

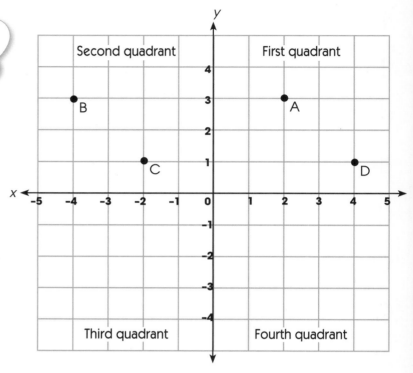

Graph the ordered pairs in each table. Then connect the points with a line.

9

x	y
–2	–4
–4	–6
–6	–8
–8	–10

10

x	y
–9	9
–8	8
–7	7
–6	6

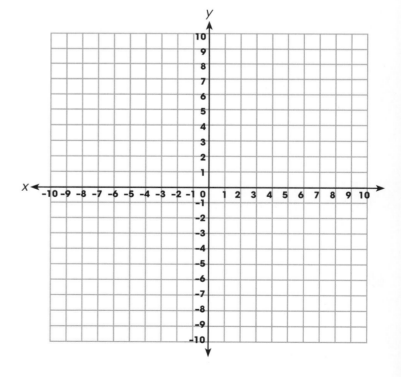

11

hours (x)	3	4	5	6
dollars (y)	5	6	7	8

☆ **Explain why the order of the numbers in an ordered pair is important. Give an example.**

●●●

Solve. Use the coordinate plane.

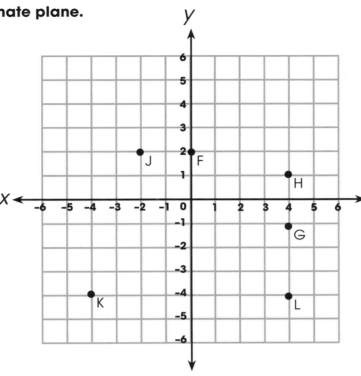

1 What ordered pair describes the location of point F?

2 What point has coordinates (–2, 2)?

3 What ordered pair describes the location of point K?

4 What ordered pair describes the location of point H?

Circle the letter for the correct answer.

5 Which point is located at (4, –1)?

a) Point L

b) Point K

c) Point H

d) Point G

6 Which point is located at (4, –4)?

a) Point L

b) Point K

c) Point H

d) Point G

Unit 15
Exponents

Expressions & Equations
Apply and extend previous understandings of arithmetic to algebraic expressions.
6.EE.1. Write and evaluate numerical expressions involving whole-number exponents.

Model the Skill

◆ Write the following chart on the board.

Exponent Form	Expanded Form	Standard Form
exponent ↓ 2^3 ↑ base	$= 2 \times 2 \times 2$ ↖ ↑ ↗ factors	$= 8$

◆ **Say**: *Today we are going to be practicing using exponents and writing numbers in standard, exponent, and expanded form. Look at the chart. Look at the column for exponents form. Which number is the base? (2) Which number is the exponent? (3) What does the exponent tell us to do? (Tells us how many times to multiply a factor by itself, in this case, multiply 2 x 2 x 2) Explain why 2^3 is equal to 8. (Because 2 x 2 = 4 and 4 x 2 = 8, therefore, 2^3 = 8).*

◆ **Ask**: *What is the expanded form of 10^3? (10 x 10 x 10) What is the standard form of 10^3? (1,000)*

◆ Assign students the appropriate practice pages to support their understanding of the skill.

Assess the Skill

Use the following problems to pre-/post-assess students' understanding of the skill.

◆ Ask students to complete the following chart.

Exponent Form	Expanded Form	Standard Form
1^3		
	5 x 5 x 5	
		64

Write each using exponents.

exponent
↓
10^3 = 10 x 10 x 10 $10^3 = 1,000$
↑   ↖ ↑ ↗
base   factors

1 10 x 10

Think: Write the number of factors as the exponent.

_____

2 10 x 10 x 10 x 10

_____

3 9 x 9

Think: 9 is the base. How many factors?

_____

4 3 x 3 x 3 x 3

_____

5 6 x 6 x 6

_____

6 12

Think: The number is in standard form. What are its factors?

_____

Write each as a number in standard form. Use a calculator.

7 9^2

_____

8 4^3

_____

9 3^5

_____

10 12^2

_____

Think: The base is 9. The exponent shows how many times the base is used as a factor.

11 10^6

_____

12 8 x 8 x 8

_____

13 20 x 20

_____

14 2 x 2 x 2 x 2

_____

 Look at the page. Draw a circle around a number that is equal to 8^3.

Name _____

Complete.

	Exponent Form	Expanded Form	Standard Form
1	base→4^3←exponent	4 x 4 x 4	
2	3^3	___ x ___ x ___	27
3		2 x 2 x 2 x 2 x 2	
4	5^2		
5			36
6		10 x 10 x 10	
7	2^5		
8		1 x 1 x 1 x 1 x 1 x 1	
9			125
10	10^5		

Write each number in standard form. Use a calculator.

11 6^3 **12** 3^4 **13** 10^4 **14** 20^3

_____   _____   _____   _____

15 4^6 **16** 7 x 7 x 7   **17** 50 x 50   **18** 5 x 5 x 5 x 5

_____   _____   _____   _____

19 8^4 **20** 3 x 3 x 3   **21** 15 x 15   **22** 2 x 2 x 2 x 2 x 2

_____   _____   _____   _____

 Tell why 4^3 and 3^4 do not have the same value.

Complete.

	Exponent Form	Expanded Form	Standard Form
1	5^2	5 x 5	
2		6 x 6 x 6 x 6	
3			64
4	10^6		
5	3^6		
6		7 x 7 x 7	
7			256
8	12^3		
9	1^6		
10		4 x 4 x 4	

Write each number in standard form. Use a calculator.

11 9^2

12 4^3

13 3^5

14 12^2

_____   _____   _____   _____

15 10^6

16 9 x 9 x 9

17 30 x 30

18 6 x 6 x 6 x 6

_____   _____   _____   _____

19 5^4

20 3^8

21 10 x 10 x 10 x 10

22 6^3

_____   _____   _____   _____

☆ **Explain how you find the value of a number written in exponent form. Give an example.**

_____

_____

Name _____

Solve. Use a calculator if you wish.

1 What is the value of $5^2 - 5^1$?

2 What is the value of $2^4 - 2^2$?

3 What is the value of $10^5 - 10^3$?

4 What is the value of $10^3 - 5^3$?

5 What is the value of $8^4 - 4^3$?

6 What is the value of $7^4 - 6^4$?

Circle the letter for the correct answer.

7 Which is the number one million in exponent form?

    a) 10^1

    b) 10^3

    c) 10^6

    d) 1^{10}

8 Which is the standard form for 5^4?

    a) 5

    b) 9

    c) 20

    d) 625

Unit 16
Order of Operations

Standard

> **Expressions & Equations**
> **Apply and extend previous understandings of arithmetic to algebraic expressions.**
> **6.EE.1.** Write and evaluate numerical expressions involving whole-number exponents.

Model the Skill

◆ Write the anagram on the board: **PEMDAS**

1) Do operations inside **P**arentheses.

2) Evaluate **E**xponents.

3) **M**ultiply and **D**ivide in order from left to right.

4) **A**dd and **S**ubtract in order from left to right.

◆ Write the following expressions on the board:

$$3^2 \times 5 + 4 \qquad\qquad 3^2 \times (5 + 4)$$

◆ **Say**: *Today we are going to be evaluating expressions by following the order of operations. What is the solution to the first expression? (49) What is the solution to the second expression? (81) Explain how the parentheses effects the outcome.*

◆ Assign students the appropriate practice pages to support their understanding of the skill.

Assess the Skill

Use the following problems to pre-/post-assess students' understanding of the skill.

$$6^2 - 9 \times 2 \qquad\qquad (6^2 - 9) \times 2$$

$$(6^2 - 4^2) \times 2 \qquad\qquad 6^2 - 4^2 \times 2$$

Name _____

Evaluate each expression.

How to Evaluate an Expression Using the Order of Operations	1) Do operations inside **P**arentheses.
	2) Evaluate **E**xponents.
	3) **M**ultiply and **D**ivide in order from left to right.
	4) **A**dd and **S**ubtract in order from left to right.

1 $4 + 2 (6 + 3^2)$ ← simplify the exponent

   $4 + 2 (6 + 9)$ ← add within parentheses

     $4 + 2 (15)$ ← multiply 2 x 15

       $4 + 30$ ← add

   _____

2 $12 ÷ 2 + 3 \times 7$ ← Divide

   _____ $+ 3 \times 7$ ← Multiply

   _____ + _____ ← Add

   _____

3 $5 (8 - 3)$

   $5 \times$ ____

   _____

> Remember: This means to multiply the value in the parentheses by 5.

4 $4^2 + 6 \times 3$

   ____ $+ 6 \times 3$

   ____ + ____

   _____

5 $(6 + 24) ÷ 5$

   _____ ÷ 5

   _____

6 $(9 + 7) - (2 \times 4)$

   _____ - _____

   _____

7 $5^2 ÷ 5$

   ___ ÷ 5

   _____

8 $26 - 2 \times 3^2$

☆ **Look at Problem 8. Draw a circle around the first thing you should do to evaluate the expression.**

Evaluate each expression. Use the order of operations.

Remember: **PEMDAS**

1) **P**arentheses   2) **E**xponents   3) **M**ultiply and **D**ivide   4) **A**dd and **S**ubtract
                                            (as it occurs left to right)   (as it occurs left to right)

1 $12 \times (4 + 6) \div 5$

    $12 \times$ _____ $\div 5$

       _____ $\div 5$

    _____

2 $32 + 5 \times 4$

    _____

3 $20 - 6 \times 2$

    _____

4 $(15 - 3) \times 5$

    _____

5 $3^2 + 5 \times 4$

    _____

6 $2^4 - 7 \times 2$

    _____

7 $10^2 - 4^2 \times 2$

    _____

8 $3^3 + 8 \times 2^2$

    _____

9 $24 - 6^2 \div 3$

    _____

10 $10^3 \div 2^2 \times 5$

    _____

11 $4^3 + 9 \times 2^2$

    _____

12 $6^2 - 4^2 \times 2$

    _____

Use parentheses to make each statement true.

13 $36 \div 6 - 2 = 9$

14 $6^2 - 3 \times 8 + 2 = 14$

15 $15 - 2 + 5 = 8$

⭐   **Look at Problem 3. Tell the steps you take to evaluate the expression.**

Name _____

Evaluate each expression.

1 $36 - 6 \times 2$

_____

2 $(4^2 + 5) \times 4$

_____

3 $(48 - 6) \div 3$

_____

4 $3^4 - 17 \times 3$

_____

5 $3^2 + 5 \times 4$

_____

6 $21 - 2^4 \div 4$

_____

7 $(24 \div 6) \times 3^3$

_____

8 $10^3 \div (5 \times 4)$

_____

9 $(20 \times 60) - 10^2$

_____

10 $36 - 6 \div 2$

_____

11 $3^2 + 18 \times 2^2$

_____

12 $6^3 - 6 \times 3$

_____

13 $125 - 5^2 \times 2$

_____

14 $7^2 \times 5 - 4$

_____

15 $(82 - 9^2) \times 2$

_____

Use parentheses to make each statement true.

16 $47 = 7^2 - 17 + 15$

17 $4 \times 19 - 17 = 2^3$

18 $5^3 - 9^2 - 3^2 = 35$

 Why is following the order of operations important? Explain. Use Problem 1 as an example.

Solve.

1 What is the value of the expression
$30 \div 5 + 6 \times 4$?

2 What is the value of the expression
$135 \times 2 - 8^2$?

3 What is the value of the expression
$72 \div (3^2 - 3) + 2^2$?

4 What is the value of the expression
$(3 \times 2^3) \div (4 \times 6)$?

5 Use parentheses to make the
following expression true.

$36 \div 6 + 2 \times 13 = 2^5$

6 Evaluate the following expression.
Tell if it is true or false.

$48 \div 2^2 + 12 = 5^2 - 1$

Circle the letter for the correct answer.

7 Which expression has a value of 4?

   a) $(21 - 3) \times (7 + 4)$

   b) $21 - 3 \times 7 + 4$

   c) $(14 \div 2) \times 3 + 4$

   d) $3 \times 7 - 14 + 4$

8 Which expression has a value of 3?

   a) $(6^2 - 3) \div (9^2 - 70)$

   b) $24 - 23 \times 3$

   c) $3^3 - 3^2$

   d) $3 \times (4^2 - 3^2)$

Unit 17
Algebraic Expressions

Standard

Expressions & Equations
Apply and extend previous understandings of arithmetic to algebraic expressions.
6.EE.2. Write, read, and evaluate expressions in which letters stand for numbers.

Model the Skill

◆ **Say**: *Today we are going to be writing, reading and evaluating expressions and solving for unknown numbers, or values.*

◆ Write the following problems and corresponding expressions on the board:

The number 3 squared minus
some number is equal to four.

$3^2 - n = 4$

The number four raised to the 2nd power,
divided by t is equal to 2.

$4^2 \div t = 2$

◆ **Ask**: *What is the solution to the first expression?* (n = 5) *What is the solution to the second expression?* (t = 8) *Explain how you found the answer.*

◆ Assign students the appropriate practice pages to support their understanding of the skill.

Assess the Skill

Use the following problems to pre-/post-assess students' understanding of the skill.

The sum of a number
and 4 divided by 6
squared is equal to 2.

5 more than the
product of 4 and some
number is equal to 33.

When $r = 42$, what is the
value of $3r - 3^3$?

Name _____

Write an expression for each. Use a variable.

A variable is a letter or symbol that represents a number.

1 6 more than *y*

y + _____

Think: Add 6 to a number, y.

2 The product of 12 and the number *n*

n x _____

Think: Multiply 12 and a number n to find the product.

3 The sum of a number *b* and 24

b + _____

Think: Add 24 and b to find the sum.

4 18 less than *x*

x – _____

Think: Subtract 18 from a number x.

5 A number *n* decreased by 5

_____

Think: What operation decreases or makes less?

6 An amount *a* divided by 3

_____

Think: what operation is stated?

Evaluate each expression using the value given for the variable.

7 12 + *n*, for *n* = 4

_____

Think: Substitute the value 4 for n.
12 + 4 = ___

8 3(*y* + 6), for *y* = 2

_____

Remember to follow the order of operations. Work inside parentheses first.

9 8^2 – *b* + 3, for *b* = 25

____ – 25 + 3

_____

Remember to follow the order of operations.

10 5*y* + 6, for *y* = 3

_____

Remember: 5y means 5 x the number y.

 Look at Problem 5. Tell what the value of the expression is, if the variable *n* has a value of 20.

Name _____

Write an expression for each.

1 17 times a number *y*

Think: *y* is a variable, it stands for a number.

17*y* or 17 x _____

2 10 more than *x*

Think: What operation should I use?

x _____

3 $\frac{x}{15}$

Remember that the fraction bar means division.

4 25 less than *x*

x _____

5 The sum of a number *b* and 24

b + _____

6 18 less than *x*

x – _____

7 A number *n* decreased by 5

_____

8 An amount *a* divided by 3

_____

Evaluate each expression. Let *a* = 4, *b* = 5, and *c* = 7

9 *c* + 20

Think: *y* is a variable; it stands for a number.

_____

10 2*b* – 3

_____

11 $a^2 + 10$

_____

12 5*a* + 8

_____

13 3*c* – 11

_____

14 $b^2 - 5$

_____

15 (*c* + 3) x *a*

_____

16 $c^2 - 3^2$

_____

17 $4 \times b^3 - 10^2$

_____

☆ **Look at Problem 15. Tell the steps you took to evaluate the expression.**

●●○

Unit 18
Apply Properties of Operations

Standard

Expressions & Equations
Apply and extend previous understandings of arithmetic to algebraic expressions.

6.EE.3. Apply the properties of operations to generate equivalent expressions. For example, apply the distributive property to the expression $3(2 + x)$ to produce the equivalent expression $6 + 3x$; apply the distributive property to the expression $24x + 18y$ to produce the equivalent expression $6(4x + 3y)$; apply properties of operations to $y + y + y$ to produce the equivalent expression $3y$.

6.EE.4. Identify when two expressions are equivalent (i.e., when the two expressions name the same number regardless of which value is substituted into them). For example, the expressions $y + y + y$ and $3y$ are equivalent because they name the same number regardless of which number y stands for.

Model the Skill

◆ Draw the following table on the board.

Property	of Addition	of Multiplication
Commutative	$a + b = b + a$	$a \times b = b \times a$
Associative	$a + (b + c) = (a + b) + c$	$a \times (b \times c) = (a \times b) \times c$
Identity	$a + 0 = a$	$a \times 1 = a$
Zero	Not applicable	$a \times 0 = 0$
Distributive	$a (b + c) = (a \times b) + (a \times c)$	

◆ **Say**: *Today we are going to be looking at the different properties we use to evaluate expressions. What does the commutative property tell us?* (We can add 2 addends or multiply 2 factors in any order and get the same result.)

◆ **Ask**: *What does the associative property tell us?* (We can group addends or factors in any way and get the same result.)

◆ **Ask**: *What does the identity property tell us?* (A number plus zero is always that number; a number multiplied by one is always that number.) *What is the distributive property?*

◆ Assign students the appropriate practice pages to support their understanding of the skill.

Assess the Skill

Use the following problems to pre-/post-assess students' understanding of the skill.

◆ Ask students to explain, or give an example for, each of the following properties: Commutative, Associative, Identity, Zero, Distributive.

Addition Properties	**Multiplication Properties**
Commutative Property (order)	Commutative Property (order)
$a + b = b + a$ $5 + 3 = 3 + 5$	$a \times b = b \times a$ $5 \times 3 = 3 \times 5$
Associative Property (grouping)	Associative Property (grouping)
$a + (b + c) = (a + b) + c$	$a \times (b \times c) = (a \times b) \times c$
$4 + (3 + 2) = (4 + 3) + 2$	$4 \times (3 \times 2) = (4 \times 3) \times 2$
Identity Property	Identity Property
$a + 0 = a$ $5 + 0 = 5$	$a \times 1 = a$ $5 \times 1 = 5$
	Zero Property
	$a \times 0 = 0$ $5 \times 0 = 0$

Distributive Properties of Multiplication over Addition
$a \times (b + c) = (a \times b) + (a \times c)$ $4 \times (2 + 3) = (4 \times 2) + (4 \times 3)$

Evaluate each pair of expressions. Let $m = 1$ and $n = 4$.

1 $m + (7 + n)$ ____
   $(m + 7) + n$ ____

Think: Substitute given values for m and n.

2 $m \times 25$ ____
   $0 \times m$ ____

Use the properties of multiplication.

3 $10 + n$ ____
   $n + 10$ ____

Use the properties of addition.

4 $8 \times (n \times 5)$ ____
   $(8 \times n) \times 5$ ____

5 $5 \times (m + n)$ ____
   $(5m + 5n)$ ____

Use the distributive property.

6 $n + 0$ ____
   $0 + n$ ____

Match each expression to an equivalent expression in the box below.

7 $3 (2 + y)$

8 $y + y + y =$ _____

9 $3 + y$

$3y$
$y + 3$
$6 + 3y$

☆ **Draw a circle around the equivalent expressions that show the commutative property.**

Name _____

Make each statement true. Use properties to help.

Property	of Addition	of Multiplication
Commutative	$a + b = b + a$	$a \times b = b \times a$
Associative	$a + (b + c) = (a + b) + c$	$a \times (b \times c) = (a \times b) \times c$
Identity	$a + 0 = a$	$a \times 1 = a$
Zero	Not applicable	$a \times 0 = 0$
Distributive	$a(b + c) = (a \times b) + (a \times c)$	

1 $16 \times y = 16$

$y =$ _____

2 $12 + 9 = n + 12$

$n =$ _____

3 $0 \times 1 = s$

$s =$ _____

4 $x \div 7 = 4$

$x =$ _____

5 $15 - 9 = r + 4$

$r =$ _____

6 $2 \times s = 18$

$s =$ _____

7 $5 \times (w + 9) = 60$

$w =$ _____

8 $a \div 8 = 2^3$

$a =$ _____

9 $(7 + b) \times 4 = 48$

$b =$ _____

10 $t \div 15 = 3$

$t =$ _____

11 $3 \times n - 4 = 11$

$n =$ _____

12 $c \times (1 + 8) = 54$

$c =$ _____

Match each expression to an equivalent expression in the box below. Evaluate each expression. Let $a = 4$, $b = 7$, and $c = 2$.

13 $2 (4a + 3b) =$ _____

_____ = _____

14 $4 (3b - 2a) =$ _____

_____ = _____

15 $4 (2a - b) =$ _____

_____ = _____

16 $(10a + 2b) \div c =$ _____

_____ = _____

$8a - 4b$

$\dfrac{10a + 2b}{c}$

$12b - 8a$

$8a + 6b$

 Tell how the Identity Property of Addition and the Identity Property of Multiplication are the same. How are they different?

Name _____

Make each statement true. Use properties to help.

1 $18 \times n = 18$

n = _____

2 $5 + (b + 6) = (5 + 7) + 6$

b = _____

3 $32 \times a = 0$

a = _____

4 $0 + c = 27$

c = _____

5 $14 + 16 = y + 14$

y = _____

6 $4(6 + n) = (4 \times 6) + (4 \times 8)$

n = _____

7 $2d - 11 = 33$

d = _____

8 $20 = 3y - 1$

y = _____

9 $(3 \times 5) + (3 \times 8) = 3(a + 7)$

a = _____

10 $6^2 = f^2 - 13$

f = _____

11 $s + 64 = 76$

s = _____

12 $10n - 50 = 10 \times (11 - 5)$

n = _____

13 $0 \times 4y = 28 \times 0$

y = _____

14 $4 \times (5 \times s) = (4 \times 5) \times 13$

s = _____

15 $32 = x^2 - 2^2$

x = _____

Match each expression to an equivalent expression in the box below. Evaluate each expression. Let $a = 1$, $b = 4$, and $c = 6$.

16 $5a + 5b + 5c =$ _____

_____ = _____

17 $a(7b - 2c) =$ _____

_____ = _____

18 $4(2a - b) =$ _____

_____ = _____

19 $4b + 4c \div a =$ _____

_____ = _____

20 $(8 + 2b) \times c =$ _____

_____ = _____

$2 \times (4 + b) \times c$

$4 \times (b + c) \div a$

$(a + b + c) \times 5$

$7ab - 2ac$

$8a - 4b$

☆ **Explain how the Distributive Property $a \times (b + c) = (a \times b) + (a \times c)$ can help you solve problems. Use $(5 \times 37) + (5 \times 3)$ as an example.**

Solve.

1 What value of *n* makes the statement true?

$$n \times (7 + 8) = (5 \times 7) + (5 \times 8)$$

2 What value of *s* makes the statement true?

$$9 + (4 + s) = 13 + 8$$

3 What value of *r* makes the statement true?

$$r^2 - 7 = 29$$

4 If *y* is equal to 4, is the equation below true or false?

$$y^2 - 7 = 4y - 7$$

5 Write an equivalent expression for $5 \times (v + 6)$.

6 Write an equivalent expression for $8a - 12b$.

Circle the letter for the correct answer.

7 Which statement is *false*?

a) You can add numbers in any order and the result is the same.

b) You can multiply numbers in any order and the result is the same.

c) You can subtract numbers in any order and the result is the same.

d) If the product of two numbers is 0, then one of the numbers must be 0.

8 Which statement is *true*?

a) You can add numbers in any order and the result is the same.

b) You can multiply numbers in any order and the result is different.

c) You can subtract numbers in any order and the result is the same.

d) If the sum of two numbers is 0, then one of the numbers must be 0.

Unit 19
Write and Solve Equations

Standard

Expressions & Equations
Reason about and solve one-variable equations and inequalities.

6.EE.5. Understand solving an equation or inequality as a process of answering a question: which values from a specified set, if any, make the equation or inequality true? Use substitution to determine whether a given number in a specified set makes an equation or inequality true.

6.EE.6. Use variables to represent numbers and write expressions when solving a real-world or mathematical problem; understand that a variable can represent an unknown number, or, depending on the purpose at hand, any number in a specified set.

6.EE.7. Solve real-world and mathematical problems by writing and solving equations of the form $x + p = q$ and $px = q$ for cases in which p, q and x are all nonnegative rational numbers.

Model the Skill

◆ Write the following problem on the board.

4 times the sum of a number n and 10 is 60.

◆ **Say**: *Look at the problem. What equation can we write to solve this problem?*

$4 \times (n + 10) = 60$

◆ Remind students that the value of each side of the equation is equal.
Ask: *What operations can you perform to help solve this equation?* (Answers may include: multiply $(n + 10)$ by 4 and solve $4n + 40 = 60$, $4n = 20$, $n = 5$; or simply divide both sides by 4 and solve $n + 10 = 15$; $n = 5$.)

◆ Assign students the appropriate practice pages to support their understanding of the skill.

Assess the Skill

Use the following problems to pre-/post-assess students' understanding of the skill.

◆ Ask students to write and solve equations for the following statements:
The sum of five and n *is equal to sixteen.*
The difference of t *minus six is equal to twenty-three.*
The product of n *plus five and two is twelve.*
The quotient of r *divided by 4 is equal to 7.*

Name _____

Write an equation for each.

1 A number *n* and 8 total 10.

> Think: What operation can you use to find a total?

2 A number *n* divided by 12 is 10.

$$\frac{n}{\square} = \underline{\hspace{1cm}} \text{ or } n \div \underline{\hspace{1cm}} = \underline{\hspace{1cm}}$$

> Remember: A fraction can represent division.

3 6 less than the product of 8 and a number *n* is 34.

$n \times \underline{\hspace{1cm}} - \underline{\hspace{1cm}} = 34$

> Think: A product is the result of multiplying.

> Think: 6 less means subtract 6.

4 3 times the sum of a number *n* and 12 is 45.

$3 \times (\underline{\hspace{1cm}} + \underline{\hspace{1cm}}) = \underline{\hspace{1cm}}$

Substitute the given value in the equation. Tell if the value of the variable is a solution. Circle yes or no.

5 $\frac{n}{14} = 7$ (Let *n* = 98)

Solution? yes/no

> Think: Is the statement true?

6 $27 = 16 + a$ (let *a* = 9)

Solution? yes/no

> Remember: Both sides of the equation must have the same value.

7 $y \times 49 = 0$ (let *y* = 1)

Solution? yes/no

8 $5(b - 3) = 25$ (let *b* = 8)

Solution? yes/no

Evaluate each formula for the given value.

9 $A = s^2$, for *s* = 6

$A = \underline{\hspace{1cm}} \times \underline{\hspace{1cm}}$

$A = \underline{\hspace{1cm}}$

10 $24d = h$, for *d* = 7

$\underline{\hspace{1cm}} \times \underline{\hspace{1cm}} = h$

$\underline{\hspace{1cm}} = h$

☆ **Draw a circle around the formula you can use to find the number of hours in 10 days.**

Name _____

Write an equation for each.

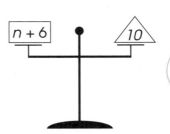

❶ The sum of a number n and 6 is 10.

_____

> Remember: The value of each side of the equation is equal.

❷ 50 less than a number n is 16.

_____ – _____ = _____

❸ 5 more than the product of a number n and 10 is 65.

_____ x _____ + _____ = _____

❹ 3 less than 16 divided by a number s is 5.

_____

❺ 6 times the sum of a number n and 4 is 54.

_____

Substitute the given value in the equation. Tell if the value of the variable is a solution. Circle yes or no.

❻ $15y = 105$ (let $y = 7$)

Solution? yes/no

❼ $6(b – 10) = 30$ (let $b = 15$)

Solution? yes/no

❽ $y \times 9 = 36$ (let $y = 3$)

Solution? yes/no

❾ $10y – 15 = 75$ (let $y = 8$)

Solution? yes/no

❿ $4(b – 8) = 16$ (let $b = 12$)

Solution? yes/no

⓫ $x \div 8 = 12$ (let $x = 96$)

Solution? yes/no

Evaluate each formula for the given value.

⓬ $P = 4s$, for $s = 12$

$P = $ _____

⓭ $D = rt$, for $r = 13$, $t = 5$

$D = $ _____

 Tell how to use the formula in Problem 12 to find the perimeter of a square with each side 25 centimeters long.

Name _____

Write an equation for each.

1 The sum of *n* and 6 total 15.

_____

2 The number *n* divided by 15 is 4.

_____

3 A number *n* is the product of 7 and 30.

_____

4 270 divided by x is 90.

_____

5 45 more than the product of 3 and a number *y* is 95.

_____

6 3 times the sum of a number *n* and 12 is 45.

_____

Substitute the given value in the equation. Tell if the value of the variable is a solution. Circle yes or no.

7 $\frac{n}{10} - 4 = 2$ (Let *n* = 60)

Solution? yes/no

8 $r \times 1 = 0$ (let *r* = 0)

Solution? yes/no

9 $8(b - 3) = 48$ (let *b* = 10)

Solution? yes/no

10 $y \times 14 = 42$ (let *y* = 3)

Solution? yes/no

11 $7(c - 3) = 21$ (let *c* = 6)

Solution? yes/no

12 $\frac{x}{3} - 7 = 0$ (let *x* = 51)

Solution? yes/no

13 $y \times 7^2 = 98$ (let *y* = 2)

Solution? yes/no

14 $5(t + 3) = 45$ (let *t* = 4)

Solution? yes/no

15 $(y - 3^2) \times 4 = 40$ (let *y* = 19)

Solution? yes/no

Evaluate each formula for the given value.

16 $P = s^2$, for *s* = 15

$P =$ _____

17 $A = lw$, for *l* = 6, *w* = 12

$A =$ _____

18 $D = rt$, for *r* = 25, *t* = 11

$D =$ _____

 Write the steps you took to determine if the value of *n* was a solution in Problem 7.

_____

Name _____

Solve.

1 What equation represents "a number y decreased by 25 is 100"?

2 Write an equation that represents "a number n increased by 25 is 100." Then solve.

---

3 If $x = 15$, what is the value of y?

$$7(x - 4) = y$$

4 If $n = 90$, what is the value of s?

$$\frac{n}{10} - 4 = s$$

---

5 Four times the sum of $g + 6$ is equal to thirty-six. What is the value of g?

6 The product of r and 9 divided by 2 is equal to twenty-seven. What is the value of r?

Circle the letter for the correct answer.

7 Which value of x makes $x - 16 = 32$ true?

a) 16

b) 26

c) 32

d) 48

8 Which equation represents "the product of a number and 12 is 108"?

a) $n + 12 = 108$

b) $n - 12 = 108$

c) $12n = 108$

d) $\frac{n}{12} = 108$

Unit 20
Write and Solve Inequalities

Standard

Expressions & Equations
Reason about and solve one-variable equations and inequalities.
6.EE.5. Understand solving an equation or inequality as a process of answering
a question: which values from a specified set, if any, make the equation
or inequality true? Use substitution to determine whether a given
number in a specified set makes an equation or inequality true.
6.EE.8. Write an inequality of the form $x > c$ or $x < c$ to represent a constraint
or condition in a real-world or mathematical problem. Recognize that
inequalities of the form $x > c$ or $x < c$ have infinitely many solutions;
represent solutions of such inequalities on number line diagrams.

Model the Skill

◆ Write the following problem on the board.

The product of a number n and 8 is greater than 16.

◆ **Say**: *Look at the problem. We cannot write an equation for this problem,
because there are an infinite number of solutions that can make that
statement true, so instead we will write an inequality. An inequality is
a statement that shows a set of values that could make the statement
true. Instead of using a symbol for "is equal to" (=), like in an equation, an
inequality uses symbols for "less than" (<) and "greater than" (>).*

◆ **Ask**: *What inequality can we write to solve this problem?*

$8 \times n > 16$

◆ **Ask**: *What operations can you perform to help solve this inequality?* (divide
both sides by 8 and solve $n > 2$).

◆ Assign students the appropriate practice pages to support their
understanding of the skill.

Assess the Skill

**Use the following problems to pre-/post-assess students' understanding of
the skill.**

◆ Ask students to write and solve inequalities for the following statements:

The sum of five and n is less than twenty.
The difference of t minus eight is greater than ten.
The product of x plus six and two is greater than twelve.
The quotient of s divided by three is less than seven.

Name _____

Write an inequality for each. Use > or <.

1 A number *n* is greater than 25.

n ◯ 25   *Think: > means is greater than.*

2 A number *n* is less than 25.

n ◯ 25   *Think: < means is less than.*

---

3 The product of a number *n* and 6 is greater than 11.

n ◯ ___ ◯ 11   *Think: "Product" is the result of multiplication.*

4 A number *n* and 4 is less than 10.

_____

Solve each inequality. Graph each solution on a number line. Then list the first three integer solutions.

5 *y* > 4

5, ___, ___

Think: An open circle means 4 is not included in the solution set: Numbers greater than 4 are to the right of 4.

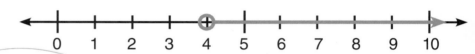

6 *y* < 4

3, ___, ___

Think: Numbers less than 4 are to the left of 4.

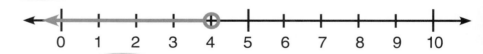

7 *n* > 6

___, ___, ___

Think: What point would you circle to start your graph?

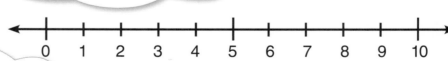

8 *b* + 3 < 7

___, ___, ___

Think: What number + 3 = 7? 3 + 4 = 7, so put an open circle on the 4. The solutions will be less than 4.

☆ **Look at Problem 5. Draw a circle around the solution set on the graph. What are all the solutions shown?**

⬤◯◯

Name _____

Write an inequality for each. Use > or <.

1 A number *n* is less than 10.

____ ◯ ____

2 The sum of a number *n* and 5 is greater than 10.

____ + ____ ◯ ____

3 A number *p* is greater than 40.

_____

4 A number *x* is less than 16.

_____

5 The product of a number *y* and 2 is less than 15.

_____

6 A number *c* divided by 3 is less than 20.

$\dfrac{c}{\Box}$ ◯ ____ or c ÷ ____ ◯ ____

Solve each inequality. Graph each solution on a number line. Then list the first three integer solutions.

7 *x* > 6

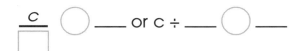

7, ____, ____

Remember: 6 is not part of the solution set, so show with open circle. Numbers to the right of a given number are greater.

8 *x* < 6

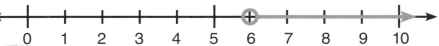

3, ____, ____

9 *b* − 1 > 5

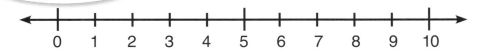

____, ____, ____

10 *b* + 4 > 7

____, ____, ____

 Look at the eighth problem. Tell how you know whether the graph should point to the right or left of 6.

Name _____

Write an inequality for each. Use > or <.

1 A number y is greater than 50.

_____

2 The sum of a number n and 9 is greater than 20.

_____

3 A number x is less than 15.

_____

4 5 less than the number n is less than 10.

_____

5 The product of a number n and 5 is greater than 10.

_____

6 A number c divided by 4 is less than 25.

_____

Solve each inequality. Graph each solution on a number line. Then list the first three integer solutions.

7 $y > 2$

____, ____, ____

8 $c < 4$

____, ____, ____

9 $x + 3 < 6$

____, ____, ____

10 $r + 3 > 8$

____, ____, ____

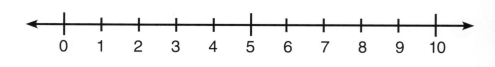

 How many solutions does an inequality have? Explain.

_____

_____

●●●

Solve.

1 A lawn service charges under $50 to mow a lawn. Write an inequality to represent the amount charged.

2 Ms. Kelly puts more than 5 apples in each bag. Write an inequality to represent the number of apples in a bag.

3 Theresa had $150. She spent more than $50 at the grocery store. Write an inequality to show the amount she has left.

4 Victor divides the oranges into 4 bowls. Each bowl has more than 8 oranges. Write an inequality to represent the total number of oranges.

5 Mr. Milo puts less than 3 books on each desk. There are 20 desks. Write an inequality to represent the total number of books.

6 Frida makes more than 4 bracelets in 2 hours. Write an inequality to represent the hourly rate at which Frida makes bracelets.

Circle the letter for the correct answer.

7 Which inequality is shown by the graph below?

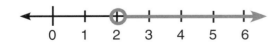

a) $n > 6$

b) $n < 6$

c) $n > 2$

d) $n < 2$

8 Which inequality is shown by the graph below?

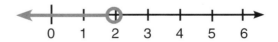

a) $x > 3$

b) $x > 2$

c) $x < 1$

d) $x < 2$

Unit 21
Graph Equations

Standard

Expressions & Equations
Represent and analyze quantitative relationships between dependent and independent variables.
6.EE.9. Use variables to represent two quantities in a real-world problem that change in relationship to one another; write an equation to express one quantity, thought of as the dependent variable, in terms of the other quantity, thought of as the independent variable. Analyze the relationship between the dependent and independent variables using graphs and tables, and relate these to the equation. .

Model the Skill

◆ Draw the coordinate plane, the corresponding table, and the following equation on the board.

$y = x - 2$

◆ **Say**: *Today we are going to be graphing equations on the coordinate plane. Look at the equation. What does the equation show?* (the equation shows that for every value of *x*, *y* is 2 less)

◆ Assist students in completing the chart and then demonstrate how to use the x,y coordinates to graph the equation and connect it to show a line.

◆ Assign students the appropriate practice pages to support their understanding of the skill.

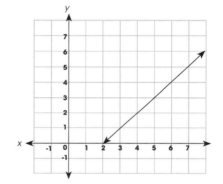

x	y
7	5
6	
5	
4	
3	

Assess the Skill

Use the following problems to pre-/post-assess students' understanding of the skill.

◆ Ask students to graph the following equations on the coordinate plane.

$y = 3x$ $2y = x$ $y - 1 = 2x$

Name 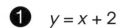 _____

Complete each table. Then graph the equation.

1 $y = x + 2$

x	y
4	6
3	5
2	
1	
0	

Think: The equation describes the relationship. For every value of x, y is 2 more.

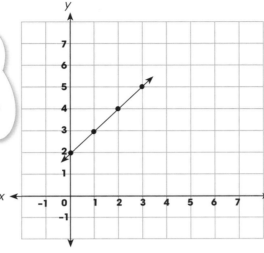

Think: Each point on the graph represents an ordered pair from the table.

2 $y = x - 3$

x	y
7	4
6	
5	
4	
3	

Think: First use the equation to find the ordered pairs and then graph them.

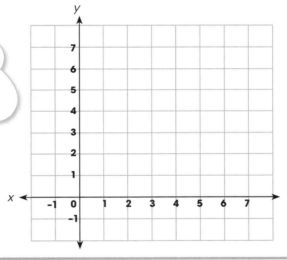

3 $D = 5t$

D	t
5	1
10	2
15	3
	4
	5

Think: $D = rt$ is a formula. The rate is 5, so distance = 5 x t.

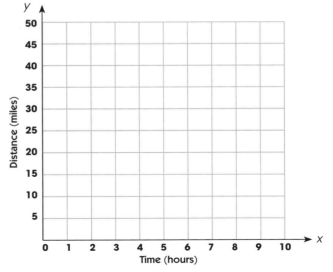

 Look at Problem 3. Make a point on the graph that shows how much time it takes to go 35 miles.

Name _____

Complete each table. Then graph the equation.

1 $y = 2x + 1$

x	y
5	11
4	
3	
2	
1	

Think: The equation shows that for every value of x, y is two times more plus 1.

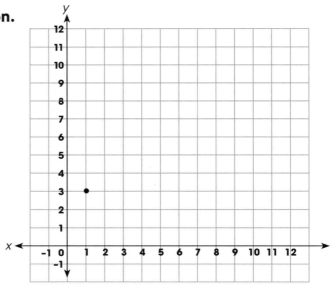

2 $y = x - 2$

x	y
7	5
6	
5	
4	
3	

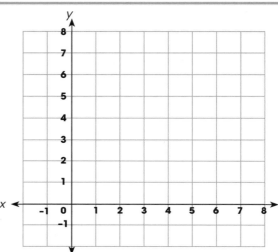

3 Cost is ticket price + $2 handling fee

t	c
4	6
6	
8	
10	
12	

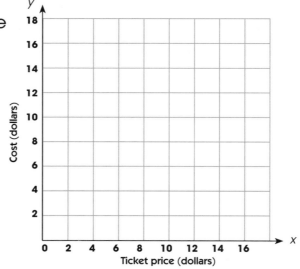

 Look at Problem 1. Tell what y will be if x = 0.

Complete each table. Then graph the equation.

1 $y = 2x + 2$

x	y
4	
3	
2	
1	
0	

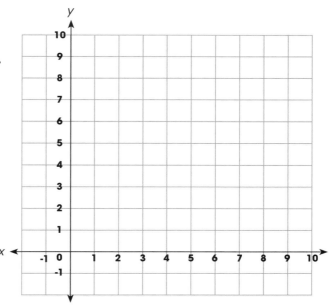

2 $y = x - 1$

x	y
8	
6	
4	
2	
0	

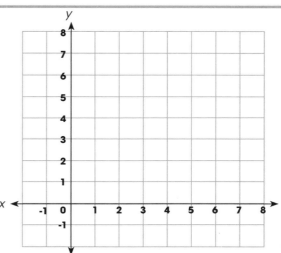

3 $D = 3t$

D	t
30	10
	20
	30
	40
	50

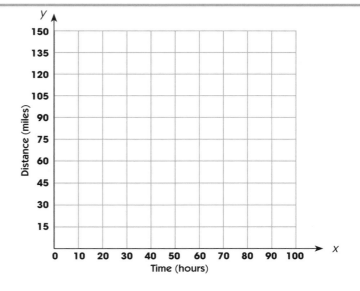

 Explain the steps you took to graph the equation in Problem 2.

_____

_____

Name _____

Solve. Use the graph for Problems 1–3.

1 What ordered pair represents point A?

(_____, _____)

2 Circle the equation that was used to create the graph.

$y = 2x$ $y = x + 2$ $y = x - 2$

3 If x is 6, what is the value of y?

_____

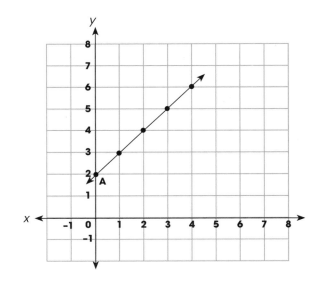

4 $x = y - 2$

x	y
4	6
3	
2	
1	
0	

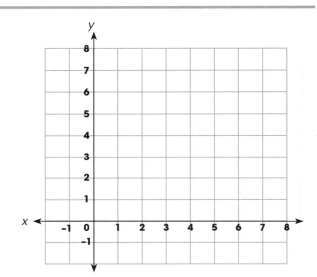

Circle the letter for the correct answer.

5 Which equation was used to create the table below?

a) $y = x + 3$

b) $y = 2x + 1$

c) $y = 3x$

d) $y = 3x - 1$

x	y
1	2
2	5
3	8
4	11
5	14

6 Which graph shows the equation $D = 2t$?

a)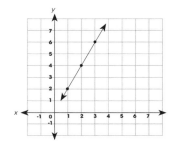

b)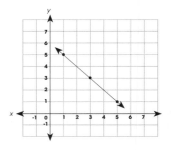

Unit 22
Area of Parallelograms and Triangles

Standard

Geometry
Solve real-world and mathematical problems involving area, surface area, and volume.
6.G.1. Find the area of right triangles, other triangles, special quadrilaterals, and polygons by composing into rectangles or decomposing into triangles and other shapes; apply these techniques in the context of solving real-world and mathematical problems.

Model the Skill

◆ Draw the following figure on the board.

◆ **Say**: *Today we are going to be finding the area of triangles and parallelograms. Look at the rectangle ABCD. What is the length of this rectangle?* (4 units) *What is the width?* (2 units). *If the formula for the area of a rectangle is A = l x w, what is the area of this rectangle?* (8 square units)

◆ **Ask**: *If the line AC cuts the rectangle ABCD in half, what do you think the area of the triangle ACD is?* (half of the area of the rectangle, or 4 square units)

◆ **Say**: *We use the formula A = 1/2 x b x h to find the area of a triangle. What is the base of this triangle ADC?* (4 units) *What is the height?* (2 units). *Use the formula to find the area.*

◆ Assist students in using the formula to find the area of the triangle and compare it to their prediction of 4 square units.

◆ Assign students the appropriate practice pages to support their understanding of the skill.

Assess the Skill

Use the following problems to pre-/post-assess students' understanding of the skill.

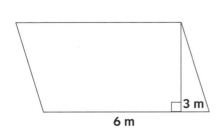
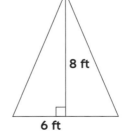
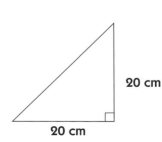

Find the area of each figure.

1 Rectangle ABCD

Area = base x height (A = bh)

A = 5 x 4

A = _____ square units

> Think: The base of a rectangle is its length. The height is its width.

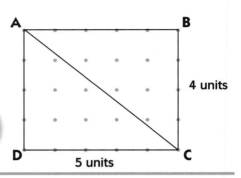

4 units

5 units

2 Triangle ABC

Area = $\frac{1}{2}$ base x height (A = $\frac{1}{2}bh$)

A = $\frac{1}{2}$ (4 x 3)

A = _____ square units

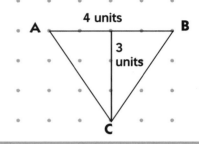

4 units

3 units

3 Triangle ADC

Area = $\frac{1}{2}$ base x height (A = $\frac{1}{2}bh$)

A = $\frac{1}{2}$ (5 x 4)

A = _____ square units

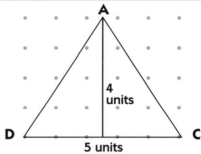

4 units

5 units

4 Parallelogram DEFG

Area = bh

A = _____ x _____

A = _____ square units

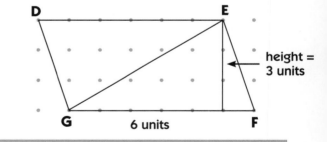

height = 3 units

6 units

5 Triangle DEG

A = $\frac{1}{2}bh$

A = $\frac{1}{2}$ (_____ x _____)

A = _____ square meters

2 m

2 m

6

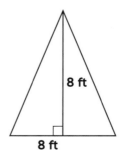

8 ft

8 ft

A = $\frac{1}{2}bh$

A = $\frac{1}{2}$ (_____ x _____)

A = _____ square feet

☆ **Look at Problem 4. Show how to make a rectangle with a base of 6 and height of 3 (Hint: Cut and rearrange the parallelogram.)**

Name _____

Use the formula *A = bh* to find the area of each parallelogram.

 1

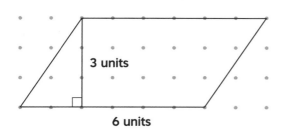

3 units

6 units

A = 6 x _____

A = _____ square units

 2

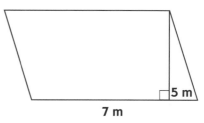

5 m

7 m

A = _____ x _____

A = _____ square meters

 3

5 units

7 units

A = _____

 4

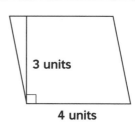

3 units

4 units

A = _____

Use the formula *A = $\frac{1}{2}$bh* to find the area of each triangle.

 5

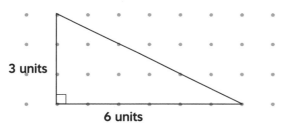

3 units

6 units

A = $\frac{1}{2}$ (6 x _____)

A = _____ square units

6

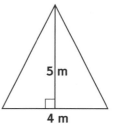

5 m

4 m

A = _____ x _____

A = _____ square meters

 7

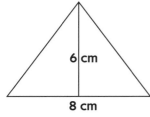

6 cm

8 cm

A = _____

8

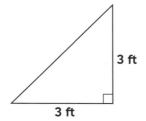

3 ft

3 ft

A = _____

 ☆ **Tell why the area of a triangle is one half the area of a parallelogram with the same base and height.**

Name _____

Use the formula $A = bh$ to find the area of each parallelogram.

1

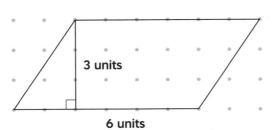

3 units

6 units

$A = 6 \times$ _____

$A =$ _____ square units

2

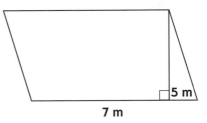

5 m

7 m

$A =$ _____ $\times$ _____

$A =$ _____ square meters

3

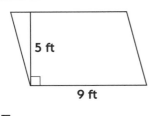

5 ft

9 ft

$A =$ _____

4

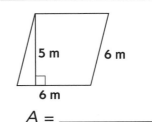

5 m   6 m

6 m

$A =$ _____

Use the formula $A = \frac{1}{2} bh$ to find the area of each triangle.

5

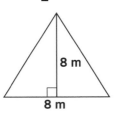

8 m

8 m

$A =$ _____

6

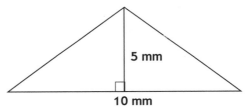

5 mm

10 mm

$A =$ _____

7

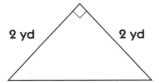

2 yd   2 yd

$A =$ _____

8

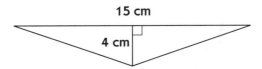

15 cm

4 cm

$A =$ _____

9

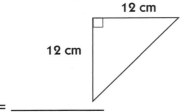

12 cm

12 cm

$A =$ _____

10

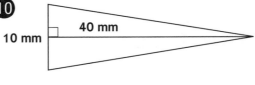

40 mm

10 mm

$A =$ _____

 Write the steps you took to solve Problem 5. Did you write your answer in square meters? Explain why or why not.

●●●

Solve.

1 Darren cut along a diagonal line across a sheet of paper to make a triangle. The paper was 10 inches long and 8 inches wide. What is the area of the triangle he created?

A = _____

2 Jaya has a 10 cm square piece of origami paper. If she folds the square into 4 equal triangles, what will be the area of each triangle?

A = _____

3 The sailboat has 1 large sail and 1 small sail. The large sail is 24 feet tall. The base of the sail is 12 feet long. What is the area of the large sail?

A = _____

4 The triangle cookie-cutter has a base of 10 centimeters and a height of 8 centimeters. What is the area of each triangle cookie?

A = _____

5 The quilt has 5 parallelograms. Each parallelogram has a base of 10 inches and a height of 7 inches. What area of the quilt is covered by the parallelograms?

A = _____

6 The parallelogram has a height of 14 centimeters and a base of 3 centimeters. What is the area?

A = _____

Circle the letter for the correct answer.

7 Which is the area of the triangle below?

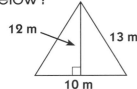

a) 60 square meters
b) 65 square meters
c) 120 square meters
d) 130 square meters

8 Which is the area of the figure BCD below?

a) 300 square meters
b) 150 square meters
c) 15 square meters
d) 30 square meters

Unit 23
Draw Polygons on the Coordinate Plane

Standard

Geometry
Solve real-world and mathematical problems involving area, surface area, and volume.
6.G.3. Draw polygons in the coordinate plane given coordinates for the vertices; use coordinates to find the length of a side joining points with the same first coordinate or the same second coordinate. Apply these techniques in the context of solving real-world and mathematical problems.

Model the Skill

◆ Draw the coordinate plane, and write the following set of coordinates on the board.

(2, 3), (2, –3), (–2, –3), (–2, 3)

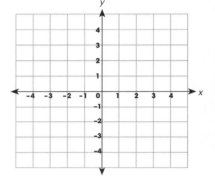

◆ **Say**: *Today we are going to be graphing polygons on the coordinate plane. Look at this set of ordered pairs. Each gives us the coordinates for a specific point on the plane. Plot each point. Then connect the points so that each point represents a vertex.*

◆ Assist students in plotting each point and then connecting the points to make a rectangle. Remind students that the coordinates are always ordered (*x, y*).

◆ **Ask**: *What type of polygon do you see?* (rectangle)

◆ Assign students the appropriate practice pages to support their understanding of the skill.

Assess the Skill

Use the following problems to pre-/post-assess students' understanding of the skill.

◆ Ask students to predict which quadrant(s) the shape will be in as well as what types of polygons the coordinates will yield. Then ask them to plot and graph each polygon using the following sets of coordinates.

(1, 3), (1, 1), (3,1)   (3, 2), (2, –3), (–3, –3), (–2, 2)

(1, 4), (1, –4), (–2, 4), (2, –4)   (–3, –1), (–1, –4), (–5, –4)

(4, –10), (–10, 4), (4, 10)   (10, –1), (1, –1), (1, –10), (10, –10)

Name _____

Graph the ordered pairs. Then connect the points in order to form a polygon.

1 Ordered pairs:

(3, 9), (9, 9), (1, 2), (7, 2)

What polygon did you draw?

_____

Remember: The first number in an ordered pair represents x.

2 Ordered pairs:

(–6, –2), (–8, –7), (–3, –7)

What polygon did you draw?

_____

Remember: To graph an ordered pair, first move across the x-axis. Then move up or down the y-axis.

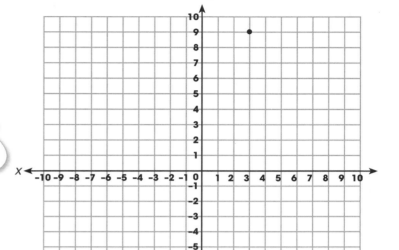

3 Complete the coordinates to draw a square on the grid below.

(–5, 4), (5, 4), (5, –6), (___, ___)

Think: What ordered pair represents the point for the fourth vertex?

4 Draw another square on the grid. What are the coordinates of its vertices?

(___, ___), (___, ___), (___, ___), (___, ___)

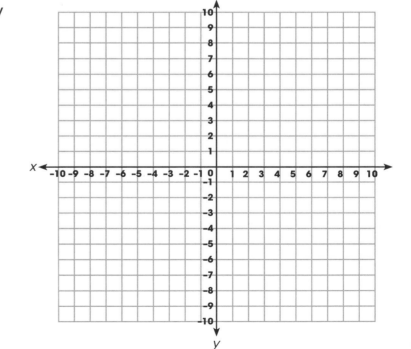

 Look at the coordinates for Problem 3. Tell how you know the figure is a square.

Name _____

Graph the ordered pairs. Then connect the points in order to form a polygon.

❶ Ordered pairs:

(4, 4), (7, 4), (1, –2), (9, –2)

What polygon did you draw?

_____

> Think: Each point represents a vertex. A quadrilateral has 4 vertices. What type of quadrilateral is this?

❷ Ordered pairs:

(–3, –2), (–3, –6), (–6, –6), (–6, –2)

What polygon did you draw?

_____

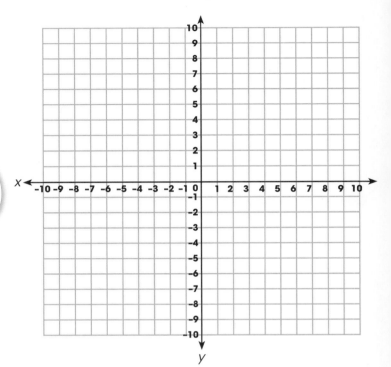

❸ Complete the coordinates to draw a square on the grid below.

(–7, –4), (–7, –8), (___, ___), (___, ___),

❹ Draw a triangle in the second quadrant. Write the coordinates of its vertices.

(___, ___), (___, ___), (___, ___)

> Think: The ordered pairs in the 2nd quadrant are (–, +).

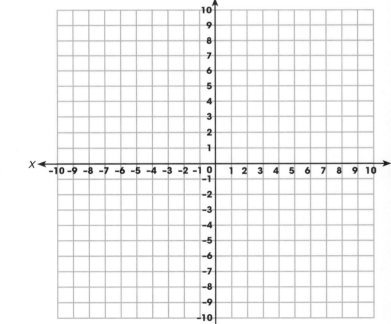

☆ **Tell how you found the missing coordinates for the rectangle in Problem 3.**

Graph the ordered pairs. Then connect the points in order to form a polygon.

1 Ordered pairs:

(–7, 6), (–3, 6), (–5, 1), (–9, 1)

What polygon did you draw?

_____

2 Ordered pairs:

(2, –3), (2, –7), (7, –5)

What polygon did you draw?

_____

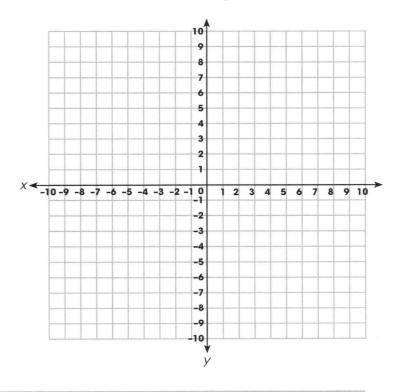

3 Complete the coordinates to draw a square on the grid.

(-5, -2), (-5, -6), (__, __), (__, __),

4 Draw a square in the second quadrant with one vertex at (-8, 6). List the coordinates for the other 3 vertices.

_____

5 Move the square you drew for Problem 4 across the y-axis into the first quadrant. List the new coordinates.

_____

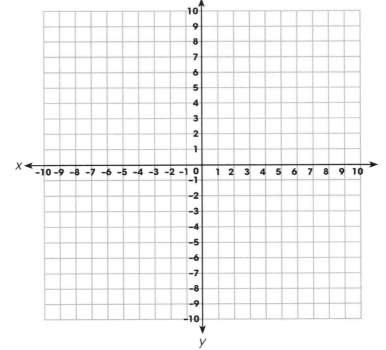

☆ **Explain what you notice about the coordinates for the square in Problems 4 and 5.**

Solve. Use the coordinate plane for the following problems.

1 What ordered pairs represent the vertices of parallelogram ABCD?

_____

2 (3, –3) represents a vertex of what shape?

_____

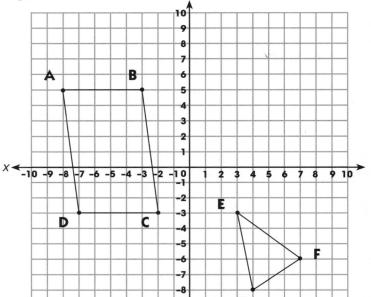

3 Draw a square in the first quadrant. List the coordinates of its vertices.

_____

4 List the coordinates for the shape in the fourth quadrant.

_____

Circle the letter for the correct answer.

5 Which ordered pairs show the vertices of a rectangle?

a) (3, 2), (2, 5), (4, 5), (5, 4)

b) (5,–6), (5, 8), (2, 8), (2, –6)

c) (6, 6), (3, 3), (9, 9), (0, 0)

d) (–11, 5), (–6, 5), (–3, –3), (–9, –3)

6 Which pair of points are exactly 5 units apart?

a) Points E and F

b) Points G and F

c) Points A and D

d) Points D and C

Unit 24
Find Surface Area

Standard

Geometry
Solve real-world and mathematical problems involving area, surface area, and volume.
6.G.4. Represent three-dimensional figures using nets made up of rectangles and triangles, and use the nets to find the surface area of these figures. Apply these techniques in the context of solving real-world and mathematical problems.

Model the Skill

◆ **Say**: *Today we are going to practice finding the surface area of different shapes.* You can use a pizza box or a gift box to remind students about the concept of surface area and that surface area is additive. **Say**: *Therefore we can use both addition and multiplication to calculate surface area.*

◆ Then draw the following solid shape and corresponding net on the board.

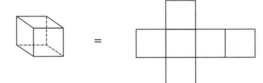

◆ **Ask**: *What type of shape is this?* (cube). *How many surfaces does it have?* (six). *This pattern, or net, shows what the cube looks like when it is flat. We can fold this net to make the cube-shaped box.*

◆ **Ask**: *If each of these flat sides has an area of 9 square units, what is the total surface are of the cube?* (54 square units). *How did you find the answer?*

◆ Assign students the appropriate practice pages to support their understanding of the skill.

Assess the Skill

Use the following problems to pre-/post-assess students' understanding of the skill.

◆ Ask students to calculate the surface area for these figures.

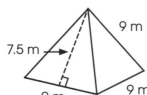

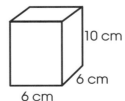

Name _____

Match the net to the solid figure it forms.

❶ 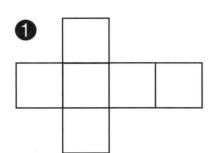   ❷ 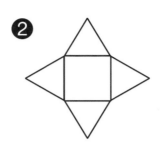   ❸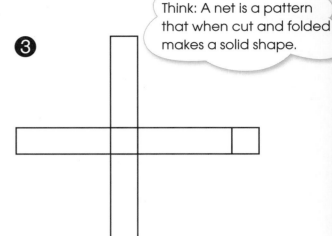

> Think: A net is a pattern that when cut and folded makes a solid shape.

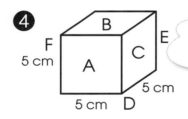

Solid Figures

 Use the nets in the first three problems to help you find the surface area of each figure.

❹

> Think: Find the area of each face. Then add.

❺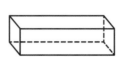

> Think: 4 faces are triangles, each with a height of 2.5 cm. 1 face is a square.

Area of Face   A: _____ x _____ = _____

B: _____ x _____ = _____

C: _____ x _____ = _____

D: _____ x _____ = _____

E: _____ x _____ = _____

F: _____ x _____ = _____

Area of Face   ____: _____

____: _____

____: _____

____: _____

____: _____

Surface Area = _____

⭐ **Show another way to find the surface area of a cube.**

Use nets to help you find the surface area of each figure.

1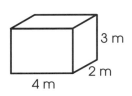

Rectangular
Prism

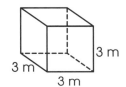 Net

Think: A rectangular prism
has 6 faces. Find the area
of each face. Then add.

Area of face 1 = _____

Area of face 2 = _____

Area of face 3 = _____

Area of face 4 = _____

Area of face 5 = _____

Area of face 6 = _____
+ _____

Surface Area = _____

2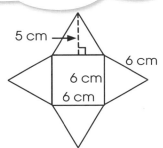

Remember to use
$A = \frac{1}{2}bh$ to find the area
of a triangular face.

Surface Area = _____

3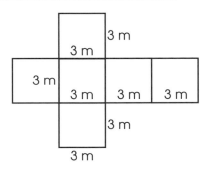

Surface Area = _____

4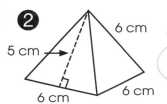

Surface Area = _____

5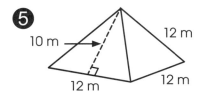

Surface Area = _____

6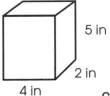

Surface Area = _____

7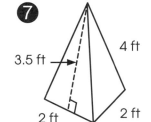

Surface Area = _____

 Tell how you found the surface area for Problem 2.

Name _____

 Use nets to help you find the surface area of each figure.

1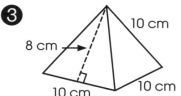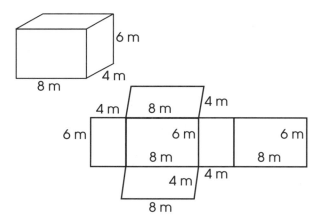

Surface Area = _____

2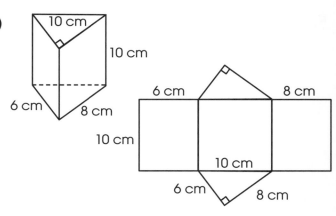

Surface Area = _____

3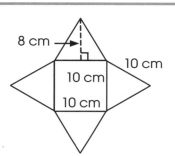

Surface Area = _____

4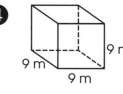
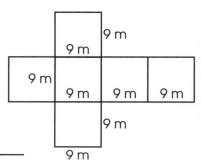

Surface Area = _____

5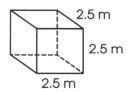

Surface Area = _____

6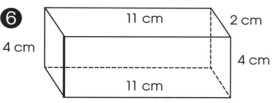

Surface Area = _____

7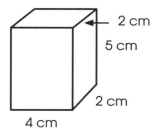

Surface Area = _____

8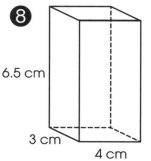

Surface Area = _____

 What is the surface area? Explain. Use Problem 2 as an example.

●●●

Solve.

1 What is the surface area of the cereal box below?

9 in

3 in

7 in

Surface Area = _____

2 What is the surface area of the recycling bin below?

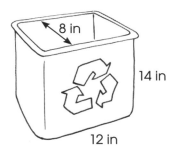

8 in

14 in

12 in

Surface Area = _____

3 What is the surface area of the trunk below?

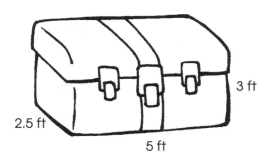

3 ft

2.5 ft

5 ft

Surface Area = _____

4 What is the surface area of the paper bag below?

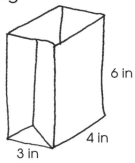

6 in

4 in

3 in

Surface Area = _____

Circle the letter for the best answer.

5 If this net were cut and folded, which solid figure would it form?

a) cube

b) pyramid

c) triangular prism

d) rectangular prism

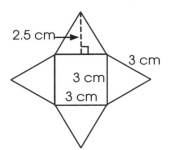

2.5 cm

3 cm

3 cm

3 cm

6 If this net were cut and folded, which solid figure would it form?

a) cube

b) pyramid

c) triangular prism

d) rectangular prism

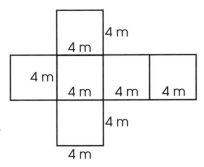

4 m

4 m

4 m

4 m 4 m 4 m

4 m

4 m

Unit 25
Find Volume

Geometry
Solve real-world and mathematical problems involving area, surface area, and volume.
6.G.2. Find the volume of a right rectangular prism with fractional edge lengths by packing it with unit cubes of the appropriate unit fraction edge lengths, and show that the volume is the same as would be found by multiplying the edge lengths of the prism. Apply the formulas $V = lwh$ and $V = bh$ to find volumes of right rectangular prisms with fractional edge lengths in the context of solving real-world and mathematical problems.

Model the Skill

◆ **Say**: *We can find the volume of different solid or three-dimensional shapes in different ways. Today we are going to be using formulas to find the volume of cubes and other rectangular prisms.*

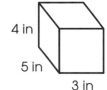

$$V = l \times w \times h$$
or
$$V = \text{Area of } base \times h$$

◆ **Say**: *Use the formula to find the volume of this rectangular prism. Remember, when we multiply to find the area, we multiply the unit x unit (unit²) , so we show our answer in square units. When we multiply volume, we multiply unit x unit x unit (unit³) so therefore we show our answer in cubic units. What is the volume?* (60 cubic inches)

◆ Assign students the appropriate practice pages to support their understanding of the skill.

Assess the Skill

Use the following problems to pre-/post-assess students' understanding of the skill.

◆ Ask students to calculate the volume for these figures.

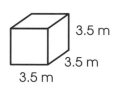

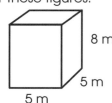

Name _____

Use the formula *V = bh* or *V = l* x *w* x *h*

①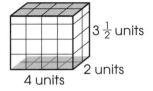

$3\frac{1}{2}$ units

2 units

4 units

Area of base: 4 x 2 = 8 square units

Height: $3\frac{1}{2}$ units

$V = bh$

$V = 8 \times 3\frac{1}{2}$

$V =$ _____ cubic units

> Think: Volume is the number of cubic units needed to fill the figure.

---

②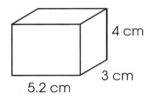

4 cm

3 cm

5.2 cm

Area of base: ____ x ____ = ____ sq. cm

$V = bh$

$V =$ ____ x 4

$V =$ ____ cubic cm

③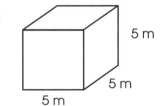

5 m

5 m

5 m

$V = l \times w \times h$

$V =$ ____ x ____ x ____

$V =$ ____ cubic meters

---

④ A rectangular box 6.8 feet long, 4 feet wide, and 2 feet high

$V =$ ____ cubic feet

⑤ A cube $3\frac{1}{2}$ inches long

> Think: The length, width, and height of a cube are the same.

$V =$ ____ cubic inches

☆ **For Problem 5, draw a picture and label it. Tell how it can help you find the volume.**

●○○

Name _____

Use the formula $V = bh$ or $V = l \times w \times h$ to find the volume of each.

1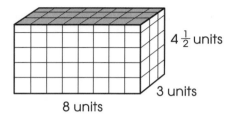

4$\frac{1}{2}$ units

3 units

8 units

Area of base: 8 x 3 = _____ square units

Height: $4\frac{1}{2}$ units

$V = bh$

$V =$ _____ x _____

$V =$ _____ cubic units

2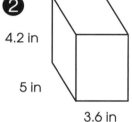

4.2 in

5 in

3.6 in

$V = l \times w \times h$

$V = bh$

$V =$ _____ x _____ x _____

$V =$ _____ cubic inches

3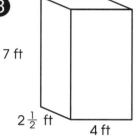

7 ft

$2\frac{1}{2}$ ft

4 ft

$V =$ _____

4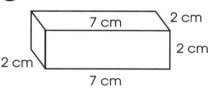

7 cm

2 cm

2 cm

2 cm

7 cm

5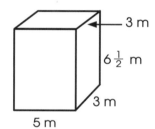

3 m

$6\frac{1}{2}$ m

3 m

5 m

6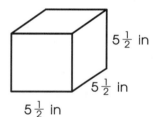

$5\frac{1}{2}$ in

$5\frac{1}{2}$ in

$5\frac{1}{2}$ in

$V =$ _____ $V =$ _____ $V =$ _____

---

7 A rectangular box 9.7 feet long, 6 feet wide, and 4 feet high

8 A cube $7\frac{1}{2}$ inches long

9 A rectangular box 11 feet long, 3 feet wide, and $5\frac{1}{2}$ feet high

$V =$ _____ cubic feet $V =$ _____ cubic inches $V =$ _____ cubic feet

 Tell which formula for finding volume you prefer to use. Tell why.

Name _____

Use the formula _V_ = _bh_ or _V_ = _l_ x _w_ x _h_ to find the volume of each.

1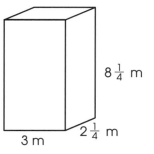

$8\frac{1}{4}$ m

$2\frac{1}{4}$ m

3 m

V = _____

2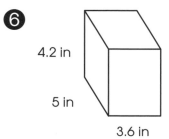

$3\frac{1}{4}$ in

$3\frac{1}{4}$ in

$3\frac{1}{4}$ in

V = _____

3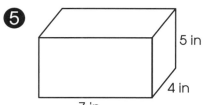

$9\frac{1}{4}$ ft

4 ft

4 ft

$2\frac{1}{3}$ ft

$9\frac{1}{4}$ ft

V = _____

4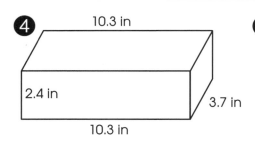

10.3 in

2.4 in

3.7 in

10.3 in

V = _____

5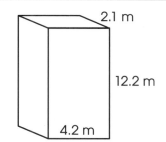

5 in

4 in

7 in

V = _____

6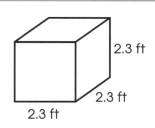

4.2 in

5 in

3.6 in

V = _____

7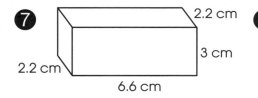

2.2 cm

3 cm

2.2 cm

6.6 cm

V = _____

8

2.1 m

12.2 m

4.2 m

V = _____

9

2.3 ft

2.3 ft

2.3 ft

V = _____

10 A rectangular box 12.7 cm long, 7.1 cm wide, and 3 cm high

V = _____ cubic cm

11 A cube $11\frac{1}{4}$ inches long

V = _____ cubic inches

12 A rectangular box 9.8 feet long, 4 feet wide, and $2\frac{1}{2}$ feet high

V = _____ cubic feet

 Look at Problem 5. How would you change the dimensions of the box to double the volume? Explain.

Name _____

Solve.

1 A locker is 1 foot long, 1 foot wide, and $4\frac{1}{4}$ feet high. What is the volume of the locker?

2 The refrigerator came in a box that was 6 feet high, 3 feet wide, and $3\frac{1}{2}$ feet deep. What was the volume of the box?

3 A pizza box is 2 inches high, $16\frac{3}{4}$ inches wide, and $16\frac{3}{4}$ inches long. What is the volume of the pizza box?

4 The feeding trough is 4 meters long, 0.5 meters wide, and 0.25 meters high. What is the volume of the trough?

5 The fish tank is 40 centimeters wide, 100 centimeters long, and 60 centimeters deep. If 1 cubic centimeter is equal to 1 milliliter, how many milliliters of water will we need to fill the tank?

6 The reflection pool is 1 meter deep, 10 meters wide, and 20.5 meters long. What is the volume of the pool?

Circle the letter for the best answer.

7 A moving company sells boxes for packing. What is the volume of the box below?

a) 360 cubic in

b) 370 cubic in

c) 380 cubic in

d) 3,600 cubic in

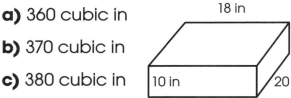

18 in

10 in   20 in

18 in

8 The suitcase is 50 centimeters long, 35 centimeters wide, and 20 centimeters deep. What is the volume of the suitcase?

a) 350 cubic cm

b) 3,500 cubic cm

c) 35,000 cubic cm

d) 350,000 cubic cm

Unit 26
Mean, Median, and Mode

Standard

Statistics & Probability
Develop understanding of statistical variability.

6.SP.1. Recognize a statistical question as one that anticipates variability in the data related to the question and accounts for it in the answers. For example, "How old am I?" is not a statistical question, but "How old are the students in my school?" is a statistical question because one anticipates variability in students' ages.

6.SP.2. Understand that a set of data collected to answer a statistical question has a distribution which can be described by its center, spread, and overall shape.

6.SP.3. Recognize that a measure of center for a numerical data set summarizes all of its values with a single number, while a measure of variation describes how its values vary with a single number.

Model the Skill

◆ Write the following definitions on the board, followed by the data set below.

  Mean: the average; the sum of all the data divided by the number of data

  Median: the middle number in an ordered set of data

  Mode: the number that occurs most often in a set of data (There can be more than one mode or no mode.)

◆ **Say**: *Today we are going to be finding the mean, median, and mode for different data sets. What is the mean?* (The **mean** is the sum of all the data, divided by the number of data.)

◆ Assign students the appropriate practice pages to support their understanding of the skill. Remind students to check and recheck their work.

Assess the Skill

Use the following problems to pre-/post-assess students' understanding of the skill.

◆ Ask students to find the mean, mode, and median for the following data sets:

$50, $35, $50, $25, $30   130, 142, 134, 140, 134, 133, 135

Name _____

Find the mean for each set of data. 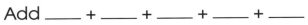 The **mean** is the sum of all the data, divided by the number of data.

1 Math quiz scores:
90, 86, 85, 93, 76

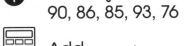 Add ____ + ____ + ____ + ____ + ____

Divide the total ____ ÷ 5

Mean = _____

Think: The mean is the average.

2 Daily high temperatures (°F):
25, 18, 30, 35, 25, 33, 30

Add __ + __ + __ + __ + __ + __ + __

Divide the total ____ ÷ ____

Mean = _____

Find the median for each set of data. The **median** of the data is the middle number when the data are arranged in order.

3 Use the data from Problem 1.
What is the median quiz score?

76, 85, ____, ____, ____

Median = _____

Think: Arrange the numbers from least to greatest. Circle the middle number.

4 State sales tax for 6 states:
6%, 8%, 3%, 5%, 6%, 7%

3, 5, ⟨6, ____,⟩ ____, ____

Median = _____%

Think: When there are two middle numbers, the median is the average of the two.

Find the mode for each set of data. The **mode** is the number that occurs most often in a set of data.

5 Points scored in a game:
3, 0, 1, 3, 4, 3, 2, 0

Mode = _____

Think: One number occurs most frequently.

6 Use the data from Problem 2.
What is the mode?

Mode = _____ and _____

Think: Two numbers occur most frequently. There are two modes.

☆ **Look at Problems 1–4. Circle the data set that has no mode.**

> **Mean (average):** the sum of all the data divided by the number of the data
>
> **Median:** the middle number in a set of data when the data are arranged in order
>
> **Mode:** the number that occurs most often in a set of data (There can be more than one mode or no mode.)

 Find the mean, median, or mode for each data set.

1 Weekly earnings of 5 dog walkers:
$48, $35, $50, $27, $25

(____ + ____ + ____ + ____ + ____) ÷ ____

Mean = $_____

$25, ____, ____, ____, ____

Median = $_____

2 Monthly rainfall (in inches):
1, 0, 3, 0.5, 0.5, 1

Mean = _____

Median = _____

> Think: Order the data to find the middle number.

> Remember: When there are two middle numbers, the median is the average of the two.

3 Annual snowfall (in inches):
20, 16, 20, 17.5, 19.5, 18, 23

Mean = _____   Median = _____

4 Foreign-language class sizes (students):
21, 20, 24, 22, 22, 22, 16

Mean = _____   Median = _____

5 Math test scores (in points):
100, 90, 72, 95, 85, 83, 89, 81, 86, 93, 98

Mean = _____   Median = _____

6 Goals per soccer game:
4, 3, 1, 1, 2, 2, 3 ,3, 2

Mean = _____   Median = _____

7 Daily low temperatures (°F):
19, 20, 18, 19, 17, 30, 17, 19

Mode(s): _____

8 Marathon times (in hours):
3.0, 3.5, 3.75, 4.25, 4.0, 3.75, 4.25, 4.5

Mode(s): _____

9 Weekly babysitting earnings:
$25, $20, $25, $35, $27, $30

Mean = _____
Median = _____
Mode(s): _____

10 Monthly electric bill:
$195, $207, $203, $245, $237, $211

Mean = _____
Median = _____
Mode(s): _____

 A newspaper reports the median house price is $250,000. From that standard, tell what you know about housing prices.

Use the report on the right to find the mean, median, and mode of the test scores for each student.

1 Scott
Mean = _____
Median = _____
Mode = _____

2 Olivia
Mean = _____
Median = _____
Mode = _____

3 Gemma
Mean = _____
Median = _____
Mode = _____

4 Chris
Mean = _____
Median = _____
Mode = _____

> **Math Test Scores Report**
> Scott: 75, 52, 80, 88, 100
> Olivia: 98, 92, 88, 92, 95
> Gemma: 84, 92, 85, 73, 86
> Chris: 88, 86, 93, 88, 90

 Find the mean, median, and mode for each data set.

5 Monthly rainfall (in inches):
1, 0, 2, 0.5, 0.25, 3, 0.25
Mean = _____ Median = _____
Mode(s): _____

6 July 4th temperatures (°F):
89, 94, 96, 99, 96, 97, 95, 92
Mean = _____ Median = _____
Mode(s): _____

7 Baby sleep log (in hours):
10, 8, 9, 8, 8.25, 9.25, 8.5
Mean = _____ Median = _____
Mode(s): _____

8 Daily running Log (in kilometers):
3.5, 0, 2.5, 5, 2.5, 3, 4.5
Mean = _____ Median = _____
Mode(s): _____

9 Reading log (in pages):
21, 42, 25, 45, 37, 34, 30
Mean = _____ Median = _____
Mode(s): _____

10 Monthly snowfall (in inches):
0.5, 2, 5, 0.25, 1
Mean = _____ Median = _____
Mode(s): _____

 Look at your answers for Problems 1-4. Which measure best describes the students' test scores? Explain. _____
_____

Name _____

Solve.

1 Sanjay has 6 math test scores. They are: 83, 80, 88, 86, 88, 70. What is the median score?

2 For the first week of December, the daily low temperatures (°F) were: 36, 40, 38, 41, 40, 32, 34. What was the mode?

3 Rachel ran 5 miles every day last week. Her running time was as follows: 39 min, 42 min, 41 min, 38 min, 39 min, 39 min, 42 min. What was her mean running time for 5 miles?

4 Ms. Krill's ten honor students scored the following grades on the pop quiz: 83, 90, 98, 96, 88, 98, 95, 97, 98, 100. What is the mode score?

5 On the bike trip, we rode 10 kilometers on Day 1, 18 kilometers on Day 2, 20 kilometers on Day 3, 15 kilometers on Day 4, and 18 kilometers on Day 5. What was the median distance we rode?

6 The rainfall for the second week in April was as follows (in inches): 1, 0, 2.5, 0.4, 0.8, 3, 0. What was the mean daily rainfall that week?

Circle the letter for the correct answer.

7 What is the mean of the data set: 20, 12, 18, 25, 20?

a) 20

b) 19

c) 18

d) 13

8 What is the mean of the data set: 112, 120, 114, 113, 118, 115, 113?

a) 113

b) 114

c) 115

d) 120

Unit 27
Make and Interpret Dot Plots

Statistics & Probability
Summarize and describe distributions.
6.SP.4. Display numerical data in plots on a number line, including dot plots, histograms, and box plots.
6.SP.5. Summarize numerical data sets in relation to their context, such as by:
   a) Reporting the number of observations.
   b) Describing the nature of the attribute under investigation, including how it was measured and its units of measurement.
   c) Giving quantitative measures of center (median and/or mean) and variability (interquartile range and/or mean absolute deviation), as well as describing any overall pattern and any striking deviations from the overall pattern with reference to the context in which the data were gathered.
   d) Relating the choice of measures of center and variability to the shape of the data distribution and the context in which the data were gathered.

Model the Skill

◆ **Say**: *Today we are using data to make dot plots. A dot plot is like a line plot, but with dots instead of X's. Look at the data. Explain how you could show this information.* Draw the following dot plot and data on the board.

Class Survey
How many sports do you play?
0, 2, 1, 3, 1, 2, 0, 3, 2,
2, 1, 2, 1, 0, 2, 1

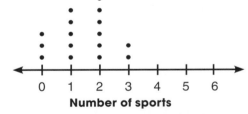

Number of sports

◆ Guide students to use the data to complete the dot plot. **Ask**: *How is it useful to represent data in this way?* (Shows people results in a clear, organized, visual way.)

◆ Assign students the appropriate practice pages to support their understanding of the skill.

Assess the Skill

Use the following problems to pre-/post-assess students' understanding of the skill.

◆ Ask students to conduct their own class survey questions, such as shoe size, height, number of siblings, etc., and then use their survey result data to make a dot plot.

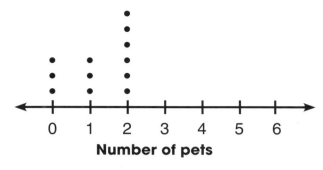

| **Class Survey** |
| **How many pets do you have?** |
| 0, 3, 1, 2, 2, 2, 0, 3, 2, |
| 4, 1, 2, 1, 0, 2 |

Number of pets

Use the survey data to complete the dot plot above. Then answer the questions.

1 How many dots should you
place above 3 on the number line? _____

> Think: Place one dot for each time 3 appears in the survey data.

2 How many students participated
in the survey? _____

> Think: Each dot represents one student.

3 What is the mode of the data? _____

> Remember: Mode is the number that occurs most often.

4 What is the mean of the data? _____

> Think: You can redistribute the dots so there is an equal number of dots above 0, 1, 2, 3, and 4.

5 What is the median of the data? _____

> Think: You can count dots to find the middle number. The eighth dot is above number 2.

6 What is the range of the data? _____

> Think: Range is the difference between the greatest number and the least number in the data.

 **What is the most common number of pets? Draw a circle around the problem
and answer that tells you. Then circle the data on the dot plot.**

Name _____

Use the dot plot to answer each question.

1 How many students participated in the survey? _____

> Think: Each dot represents one student.

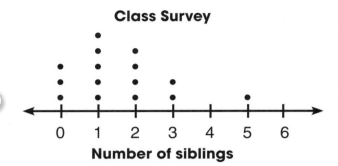

Class Survey

Number of siblings

2 What is the range of the data?

_____

> Think: Subtract the least number from the greatest number (5–0). The difference is range.

3 What is the mode of the data?

_____

4 What is the median of the data?

_____

Use the data to make a dot plot. Then answer each question.

5

Class Survey
How many sports do you play?
3, 2, 3, 4, 4, 1, 0, 2, 2,
3, 0, 2, 1, 4, 2

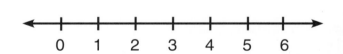

0 1 2 3 4 5 6

6 How many dots should you place above 3 on the number line?

_____

7 What number occurs most frequently? _____

8 How many students participated in the survey? _____

9 What is the mean of the data?

_____

☆ **Look at Problem 4. Tell how you found the median. Use the median to make a statement about the data: "The survey shows . . ."**

Use the dot plot to answer each question.

1 What is the range of the data?
_____

2 What is the median of the data?
_____

3 What is the mode of the data?
_____

4 Of the three measures above, which describes the data best? Why?
_____

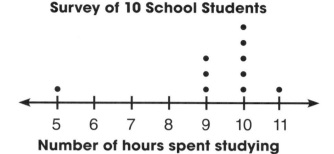

Survey of 10 School Students

Number of hours spent studying each week

Use the data to make a line plot. Then answer each question.

Class Survey
How many hours do you study?
6, 2, 5, 4, 4, 1, 2, 2,
3, 5, 2, 1, 5, 2

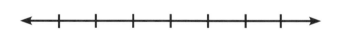

5 What number occurs most frequently? _____

6 What is the mode of the data?
_____

7 What is the mean of the data?
_____

8 What is the range of the data?
_____

9 What is the median of the data?
_____

10 Of the measures above, which describes the data best? Why?
_____
_____

 What is the average number of hours spent studying according to the survey data at the top of the page? Explain how you found the mean.
_____
_____

Name _____

Solve. Use the dot plot.

1 What is the range of scores on Sam's math quizzes?

2 Looking at Sam's math quiz scores, what is the mode?

3 What is the median score?

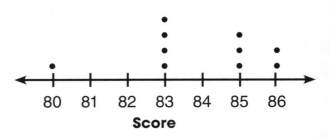

Sam's Math Quiz Scores

Score

---

4 What is the mean household size on Cedar Circle?

5 What are the modes?

6 What is the median?

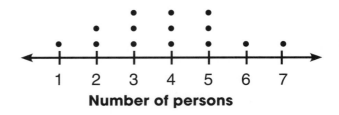

Cedar Circle Household Size

Number of persons

Circle the letter for the correct answer.

7 Which statement is true based on the data in the line plot?

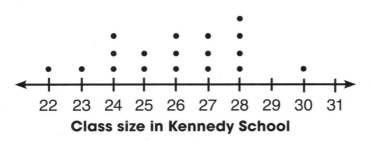

Class size in Kennedy School

a) Class size ranges from 22 to 31.

b) Half of the classes have 26 students.

c) The most common class size is 28.

8 Which statement is true based on the data in the line plot?

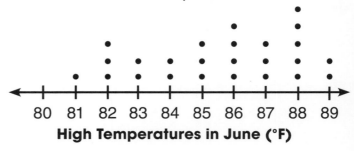

High Temperatures in June (°F)

a) The temperature in June ranges from 80 to 89.

b) The least common temperature in June is 81.

c) The most common high temperature is 88.

Unit 28
Make and Interpret Histograms

Statistics & Probability
Summarize and describe distributions.

6.SP.4. Display numerical data in plots on a number line, including dot plots, histograms, and box plots.

6.SP.5. Summarize numerical data sets in relation to their context, such as by:
   a) Reporting the number of observations.
   b) Describing the nature of the attribute under investigation, including how it was measured and its units of measurement.
   c) Giving quantitative measures of center (median and/or mean) and variability (interquartile range and/or mean absolute deviation), as well as describing any overall pattern and any striking deviations from the overall pattern with reference to the context in which the data were gathered.
   d) Relating the choice of measures of center and variability to the shape of the data distribution and the context in which the data were gathered.

Model the Skill

◆ **Say**: *Today we will use data to make histograms. A histogram is like a bar graph, but it is used to show frequency and ranges of data.* Draw the following histogram and data on the board.

Frequency Table

Ages	Frequency
1–10	15
11–20	25
21–30	20
31–40	10
41–50	10
51–60	5

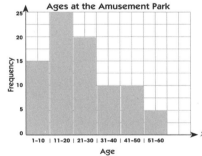

◆ **Ask**: *How is it useful to represent data in this way?* (shows people results in a clear, organized, visual way) *What does this graph tell you about who uses the park?*

◆ Assign students the appropriate practice pages to support their understanding of the skill.

Assess the Skill

Use the following problems to pre-/post-assess students' understanding of the skill.

◆ Ask students to conduct their own school-wide survey, such as date of birth ranges, and then use their survey result data to make a histogram.

Name _____

Use the frequency table to complete the histogram below, then answer the questions.

Frequency Table

Weight in pounds	Frequency
1–10	2
11–20	1
21–30	4
31–40	4
41–50	5
51–60	4
61–70	3

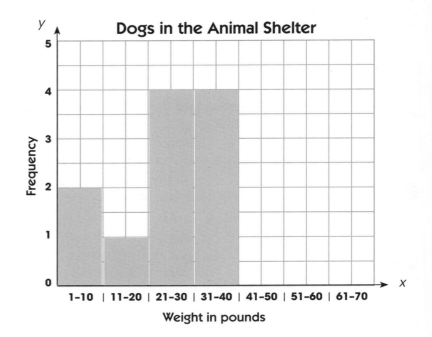

Dogs in the Animal Shelter

1 How high should you make a bar for dogs in the 41–50 lb interval? _____

Think: The frequency is 5, so the bar should match the frequency.

2 What does each interval represent? _____

Think: Each interval is an equal number of pounds.

3 How many dogs are in the shelter? _____

Think: The frequency represents the number of dogs in each interval.

4 What is the range of weight of dogs in the shelter? _____

Think: Range is the difference between the greatest number and the least number 70–1.

5 What is the most common weight of dogs in the shelter? _____

Think: Find the mode. One interval has the greatest frequency.

 All histograms include a number line. Look at the histogram. Draw a circle around the number line.

Use the histogram to answer each question.

1 How many vehicles traveled through the school intersection from noon to 2 P.M.? _____

2 How many vehicles were counted at the intersection from 8 A.M. to 4 P.M.? _____

3 What time of day was the heaviest traffic? _____

4 What is the range of time the data covers? _____

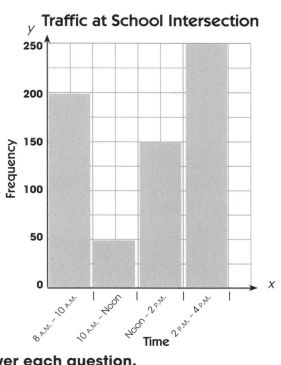

Traffic at School Intersection

Use the frequency table to make a histogram. Then answer each question.

Frequency Table

Ages	Frequency
1–10	30
11–20	15
21–30	10
31–40	15
41–50	5
51–60	10
61–70	25

5 What was the most common age group at the park? _____

6 What was the least common age group? _____

7 What is the range of ages at the park? _____

8 What two age groups visit the park most frequently? _____

 In a histogram, frequency is shown on a number line. Tell what frequency represents.

Name _____

Use the histogram to answer each question.

1. What does each interval represent?

   _____

2. How many cats are in the shelter?

   _____

3. What is the range of weight of cats in the shelter? _____

4. What is the most common weight range of cats in the shelter?

   _____

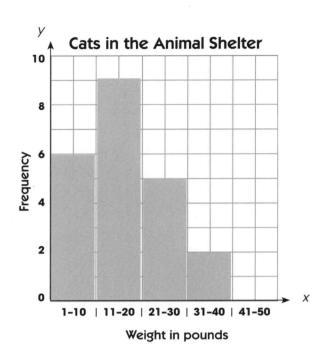

Use the frequency table to make a histogram. Then answer each question.

Frequency Table

Times	Number of Cars
8 A.M. – 10 A.M.	150
10 A.M. – Noon	100
Noon – 2 P.M.	300
2 P.M. – 4 P.M.	250
4 P.M. – 6 P.M.	350
6 P.M. – 8 P.M.	200

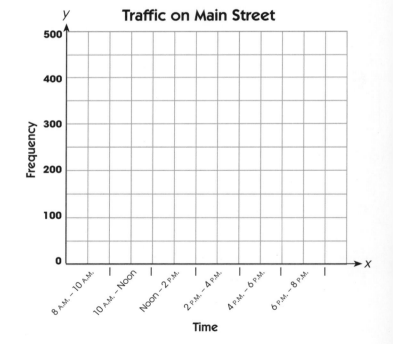

5. How many vehicles travel on Main Street from noon to 2 P.M.?

   _____

6. How many vehicles were counted on Main Street from 8 A.M. to 8 P.M.?

   _____

7. What time of day was the heaviest traffic? _____

8. What is the range of time the data covers? _____

☆ **Explain how you use data from a frequency table to make a diagram.**

Solve. Use the histogram below for the following problems.

1 What is the range of scores on the math test?

2 What is the most common range of scores?

3 What is the least common range of scores?

4 How many students took the math test?

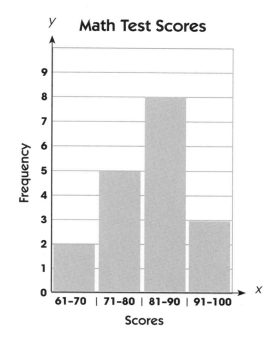

5 How many students scored above 90?

6 How many students scored below 90?

Circle the letter for the correct answer.

7 How many students scored above 80 on the math test?

    a) 16

    b) 11

    c) 8

    d) 3

8 How many students scored 71 or above?

    a) 16

    b) 11

    c) 8

    d) 3

Unit 29
Make and Interpret Box Plots

Standard

Statistics & Probability
Summarize and describe distributions.
6.SP.4. Display numerical data in plots on a number line, including dot plots, histograms, and box plots.
6.SP.5. Summarize numerical data sets in relation to their context, such as by:
    a) Reporting the number of observations.
    b) Describing the nature of the attribute under investigation, including how it was measured and its units of measurement.
    c) Giving quantitative measures of center (median and/or mean) and variability (interquartile range and/or mean absolute deviation), as well as describing any overall pattern and any striking deviations from the overall pattern with reference to the context in which the data were gathered.
    d) Relating the choice of measures of center and variability to the shape of the data distribution and the context in which the data were gathered.

Model the Skill

◆ Draw the following box plot (also known as a box and whisker plot) on the board. **Say**: *Today we are going to be making box plots. A box plot is a type of graph that shows how the data in a set are distributed.*

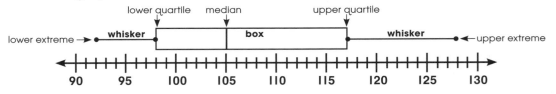

◆ Explain that to make a box plot, they must first order their data from least to greatest. Then find the lower extreme, the upper extreme, the lower quartile, the upper quartile, and the middle quartile. The lower and upper extremes are the least and the greatest numbers in the data set. The middle quartile is the median. The lower quartile is the median of the lower half of the data set. The upper quartile is the median of the upper half of the data set.

◆ Practice plotting data sets. Then assign students the appropriate practice pages to support their understanding of the skill.

Assess the Skill

Use the following problems to pre-/post-assess students' understanding of the skill.

◆ Ask students to conduct their own height survey and then use their survey result data to make a box plot.

Answer each question. Use the data to complete the box plot.

91, 95, 98, 100, 101, 105, 109, 114, 117, 120, 128

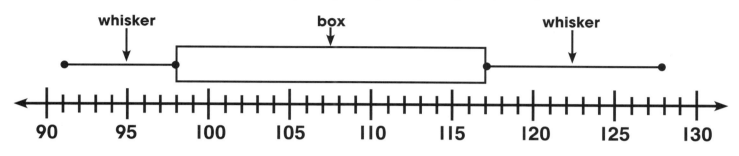

1 What is the least value of the data? _____ Label it as Point A on the box plot.

2 What is the greatest value of the data? _____ Label it as Point B on the box plot.

3 What is the median of the data? _____ Circle the median. Then show it on the box plot.

> Think: Divide the box with a line to show where the median is.

4 Circle the 5 scores below the median on the data set. What is the median of those 5 scores? _____ This is called the lower quartile. Label it Q1 on the box plot.

5 Circle the 5 scores above the median on the data set. What is the median of those 5 scores? _____ This is called the upper quartile. Label it Q3 on the box plot.

6 What is the interquartile range? _____

> Think: The interquartile range is the difference between the value of upper and lower quartiles. 117–98

☆ **Circle the whiskers on the box plot. Then circle the numbers they represent in the data set. Tell what you notice.**

Name _____

Use the data to complete the box plot. Then answer each question.

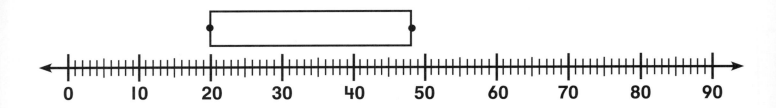

Daily Miles Traveled to and from Work
90, 18, 27, 35, 20, 5, 40, 38, 25, 48, 60

1 Put the data in order from least value to greatest value.

____ ____ ____ ____ ____ ____ ____ ____ ____ ____ ____

2 Mark the extreme values on the box plot.
Draw the whiskers.

Think: The extremes are the least value and the greatest value. Whiskers are lines that connect the extremes to the box.

3 What is the median of the data? _____
Draw the median on the box plot.

Think: Draw a line to divide the box to mark the median.

4 What is the lower quartile? _____

Think: The median of the lower half of the data

5 What is the upper quartile?

_____

6 What is the median distance

traveled? _____

7 Half of the commuters traveled between _____ and _____ miles.

8 What is the interquartile range?

_____

☆ **Tell what the box represents in a box plot.**

Name _____

Use the data to complete the box plot. Then answer each question.

Exam Scores: 91, 65, 88, 99, 63, 75, 94, 84, 100, 93, 78

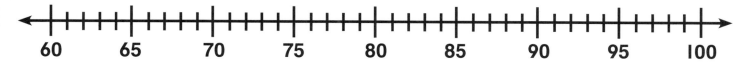

1 What is the lower extreme of the data? _____

2 What is the upper extreme of the data? _____

3 What is the median of the data? _____

4 What is the lower quartile? _____

5 What is the upper quartile? _____

6 What is the interquartile range? _____

7 Half of the class scored between _____ and _____.

8 What was the range of scores on the exam?

 Write how you determine the upper and lower quartiles and the interquartile range. What do these values tell you about the data?

_____

_____

_____

Name _____

Solve. Use the data to make a box plot, then answer the questions.

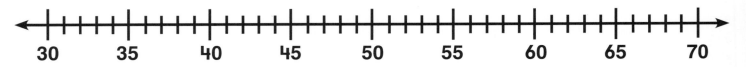

| 30 | 35 | 40 | 45 | 50 | 55 | 60 | 65 | 70 |

Daily Low Temperatures in April
36, 48, 47, 45, 40, 57, 40, 48, 45, 48, 41

1 What is the lower extreme of the data? _____

2 What is the upper extreme of the data? _____

3 What is the median of the data?
_____

4 What is the lower quartile?
_____

5 What is the upper quartile?
_____

6 What is the interquartile range?
_____

Circle the letter for the correct answer.

7 The box plot shows daily high temperatures in July (°F).

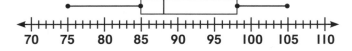

| 70 | 75 | 80 | 85 | 90 | 95 | 100 | 105 | 110 |

Half of the data are between which two numbers?

a) 85 and 98

b) 75 and 85

c) 98 and 105

d) 88 and 98

8 The box plot shows daily low temperatures in January (°F).

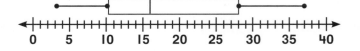

| 0 | 5 | 10 | 15 | 20 | 25 | 30 | 35 | 40 |

What was the highest low temperature for January?

a) 3°F

b) 10°F

c) 37°F

d) 40°F

Answer Key • Units 1–3

Unit 1 (p. 7) •
1. 2:5
2. 4:12
3. 3:4
4. 3:5
5. 8:10; 8/10
6. 3/3; 2/3
7. 9, 12; 8, 16, 20; 8; 20
8. 5, 10; 12, 18; 5; 18

Unit 1 (p. 8) ••
1. 5:15   **2.** 6:5
3. 5:4   **4.** 4:6
5. 3:8   **6.** 3:5
7. 1/3   **8.** 2/10
9. 1/2   **10.** 6/8
11. 8/9   **12.** 2/3
13. 1/5   **14.** 3/4
15. 10/16   **16.** 4/6
17. 3/5   **18.** 5/6

Unit 1 (p. 9) •••
1. 7:6, 6:7, 1:26
2. 10:3, 3:5, 1:2
3. 1:3, 3:55, 1:55
4. 11:10, 10:11, 1:21
5. 6, 8; 20, 40, 50; 1:5
6. 4, 8; 12, 18; 2:3
7. 1/3   **8.** 1/5
9. 7/8   **10.** 1/2
11. 2/3   **12.** 1/2
13. 1/3   **14.** 2/3
15. 4/5   **16.** 3/4
17. 3/4   **18.** 20/21

Unit 1 (p. 10)
Word Problems
1. 2:3
2. 1:1
3. 2:3
4. 1:5
5. 2:3
6. 1:4
7. C
8. D

Unit 2 (p. 12) •
1. 16, 2, 32; 2
2. 5, 6, 6
3. 21, 1, 7
4. 3:36, 1/12
5. 75 miles   **6.** 56 km
7. 12 ft   **8.** 6 mph
9. 6.4 h   **10.** 2 h
11. 2.25 h   **12.** 160 km
13. 90 km
14. 25 mph

Unit 2 (p. 13) ••
1. 25, 2; 25:1; 25 km
2. 1 for $6
3. 1:20   **4.** 1:$9.20
5. 1:60   **6.** 1:2
7. 1:30   **8.** 1:8
9. 1 for $5   **10.** 1:60
11. 1 for $0.10   **12.** 1:6
13. 100 mi   **14.** 120 km
15. 320 km   **16.** 10 hr
17. 1 hr   **18.** 2 hr
19. 105 mph   **20.** 20 kph
21. 10 m/sec

Unit 2 (p. 14) •••
1. 4:1   **2.** 1:8
3. 2:1   **4.** 6/1
5. 4/1   **6.** 7/1
7. 1:$11.33   **8.** 3:1
9. 1:$0.40   **10.** 440 mi
11. 120 mi   **12.** 150 km
13. 6 hr   **14.** 20 hr
15. 5 hr   **16.** 50 mph
17. 5 kph   **18.** 2 m/sec
19. 1 mi/min or 60 mph
20. 17 km/min or 1,020 kph
21. 40 m/min or 2,400 m/hr

Unit 2 (p. 15)
Word Problems
1. 5 for $1.00; 20 cents
2. 10 for $3.00; 30 cents
3. dozen for $7.00
4. supermarket
5. 100 hr
6. 50 cars/hr
7. B
8. D

Unit 3 (p. 17) •
1. 10%
2. 75%
3. 50%
4. 1%
5. 100%
6. 37%
7. 0.14; 14%
8. 0.25; 25%
9. 0.52; 52%
10. 0.3; 30%

Unit 3 (p. 18) ••
1. 42%   **2.** 1%
3. 30%   **4.** 75%
5. 36%   **6.** 0.5; 50%
7. 0.65; 65%   **8.** 0.03; 3%
9. 0.08; 8%   **10.** 0.5; 50%
11. 0.12; 12%   **12.** 0.05; 5%
13. 0.42; 42%   **14.** 0.01; 1%
15. 0.07; 7%
16. 0.58; 58%
17. 0.23; 23%
18. 0.09; 9%
19. 0.15; 15%
20. 0.04; 4%
21. 0.75; 75%

Unit 3 (p. 19) •••
1. 0.42   **2.** 0.01
3. 0.36   **4.** 0.60
5. 0.25   **6.** 0.50
7. 0.25; 25%
8. 0.60; 60%
9. 0.30; 30%
10. 0.50; 50%
11. 7/10; 70%
12. 20/100; 20%
13. 8/100; 8%
14. 65/100; 65%
15. .50/100; 0.50
16. 90/100; 0.90
17. 2/100; 0.02
18. 100/100; 1.00

Unit 3 (p. 20)
Word Problems
1. 65%
2. 80%
3. 20%
4. 25%
5. 60%
6. 40%
7. B
8. C

Answer Key • Units 4–6

Unit 4 (p. 22) •
1. 40%
2. 36%
3. 15%
4. 20%
5. 70%
6. 40
7. 30
8. 50
9. .375
10. 83 1/3

Unit 4 (p. 23) ••
1. 25% **2.** 10%
3. 80% **4.** 16%
5. 33 1/3% or 33.3%
6. 62.5%
7. 75% **8.** 75%
9. 37% **10.** 8%
11. 60% **12.** 37.5%
13. 1/2; 50%
14. 0.2; 20%
15. 1/3; 0.33
16. 0.80; 80%
17. 0.375; 37.5%
18. 7/8; 0.875
19. 0.16; 16.66%
20. 3/5; 0.60

Unit 4 (p. 24) •••
1. 20% **2.** 50%
3. 25% **4.** 20%
5. 75% **6.** 2.5%
7. 66 2/3% or 66.6%
8. 48% **9.** 21%
10. 6% **11.** 90%
12. 42.5% **13.** 100%
14. 49% **15.** 80.3%
16. 99.9% **17.** 2/5; 40%
18. 0.6; 60% **19.** 1/3; 0.33
20. 2/3; 66.66%
21. 0.33; 33.33%
22. 29/100; 0.29
23. 0.25; 25%
24. 21/40; 52.5%

Unit 4 (p. 25)
Word Problems
1. 3/4
2. 75%
3. 36%
4. 1:4
5. Yes; 4/5 = 0.8 = 80%
6. No; 0.6% = 0.006
7. A
8. C

Unit 5 (p. 27) •
1. 10; $10; $30
2. 3.24; $3.24; $57.24
3. 0.1; 0.1 x 250 = $25
4. 0.15; 0.15 x 80 = $12
5. 0.08 x 125 = 10
6. 0.5 x 428 = 214
7. .333 x 96 = $31.97
8. 0.45 x 540 = 243
9. 0.18 x 36 = $6.48
10. 0.20 x 100 = 20

Unit 5 (p. 28) ••
1. 40 **2.** 40.5 **3.** 30
4. 21 **5.** 3 **6.** 22.5
7. 14.5 **8.** 16
9. 266 **10.** 18
11. 9.6 **12.** 16,500
13. 34 **14.** 600
15. $14; $42
16. $6.85; $61.65
17. $30; $45
18. $66.66; $133.33
19. $40; $20

Unit 5 (p. 29) •••
1. 2.5 **2.** 75 **3.** 2.7
4. 50 **5.** 15 **6.** 90
7. 5.7 **8.** 8 **9.** 0.7
10. 31.5 **11.** 200 **12.** 990
13. 0.75 **14.** 510 **15.** 7.5
16. 5.125
17. $1.20; $22.80
18. $56.50; $45.20
19. $29.99; $60.01
20. $30; $45
21. $300; $270

Unit 5 (p. 30)
Word Problems
1. $4.50
2. 30
3. $69.60
4. 1,420
5. 51
6. $56
7. C
8. D

Unit 6 (p. 32) •
1. 7 **2.** 2
3. 1; 1,062.5 **4.** 1; 1,846
5. 80 R2 **6.** 320 2/5
7. 2,625.5 **8.** $432.75
9. 25 **10.** 318
11. 10,005 **12.** 1,060
13. 114.5

Unit 6 (p. 33) ••
1. 267 R1 **2.** 651 3/7
3. 575 **4.** 1,682 1/5
5. 304 **6.** 319.7
7. 57 2/3 **8.** 850 1/4
9. 106.25 **10.** 67.25
11. 79.2 **12.** 411.5
13. 12.8 **14.** 23
15. 15.05 **16.** 18.5

Unit 6 (p. 34) •••
1. 106 1/4 **2.** 58
3. 68 1/4 **4.** 52 1/3
5. 12 4/5 **6.** 56 2/5
7. 1,746 **8.** 678 1/2
9. 31.25 **10.** 95.38
11. 191.25 **12.** 19.88
13. 471.5 **14.** 553
15. 69.3 **16.** 18.75

Unit 6 (p. 35)
Word Problems
1. $14.25
2. 42
3. 63
4. 0.23 ft
5. 11
6. 36
7. D
8. B

Answer Key • Units 7–9

Unit 7 (p. 37) •
1. 0.63
2. 1.31
3. 0.67
4. 0.32
5. 2.15
6. 1.14
7. 4.020
8. 3.438

Unit 7 (p. 38) ••
1. 1.96   **2.** 1.05
3. 3.099   **4.** 0.598
5. 4.46   **6.** 0.5
7. 0.129   **8.** 3.837
9. 3.46   **10.** 2.10
11. 2.34   **12.** 5.10
13. 1.09   **14.** 2.12
15. 3.472   **16.** 4.597

Unit 7 (p. 39) •••
1. 1.27   **2.** 1.02
3. 2.3   **4.** 1.181
5. 2.9   **6.** 3.74
7. 2.195   **8.** 1.43
9. 1.62   **10.** 2.07
11. 2.36   **12.** 2.848
13. 0.16   **14.** 0.16
15. 1.33   **16.** 0.97
17. 5.83   **18.** 1.33
19. 0.96   **20.** 0.25
21. 6.155   **22.** 3.30
23. 0.065   **24.** 1.571

Unit 7 (p. 40)
Word Problems
1. $56.50
2. $1.49
3. $22.24
4. 8.15 ounces
5. $27.75
6. 3.5 miles
7. D
8. C

Unit 8 (p. 42) •
1. 0.12
2. 1.26
3. 0.084
4. 0.4032
5. 4.8; 48; 480
6. 2.15; 21.5; 215
7. 25
8. 4.2
9. 6.45
10. 21.25

Unit 8 (p. 43) ••
1. 0.42   **2.** $13.68
3. $0.2275   **4.** 0.2168
5. 0.072
6. 1.35; 13.5; 135
7. 1.152   **8.** 2.22
9. 10.24   **10.** 10.5
11. 2   **12.** 4.32
13. 6.45   **14.** 30.625
15. 70

Unit 8 (p. 44) •••
1. 0.108   **2.** 0.516
3. $36.24   **4.** $1.59
5. 3.796   **6.** 1.273
7. 2.7; 27; 270
8. 4.5   **9.** 120
10. 300   **11.** 16.284
12. 12.397   **13.** 204
14. 59.565   **15.** 4,100
16. 25
17. 32.2   **18.** 5
19. 8.05   **20.** 13.36

Unit 8 (p. 45)
Word Problems
1. $2.48
2. 6
3. 26.25 ounces
4. $14.95
5. $4.80
6. $15.60
7. A
8. B

Unit 9 (p. 47) •
1. 1, 2, 3, 6
2. 1, 2, 3, 4, 6, 12
3. 1, 2, 3, 6
4. 6
5. 1, 3, 5, 15;
    1, 2, 4, 5, 10, 20
6. 5
7. 9, 12, 15
8. 15, 20, 25
9. 1
10. 4, 8, 12, 16;
     6, 12, 18, 24
11. 1

Unit 9 (p. 48) ••
1. (1, 2, 4, 8); (1, 2, 3, 4, 6, 12); 4
2. (1, 3, 9); (1, 3, 5, 15); 3
3. (1, 2, 4); (1, 2, 3, 6); 2
4. (1, 2, 3, 6); (1, 2, 5, 10); (1, 2, 4, 7, 14, 28); 2
5. (1, 2, 3, 4, 6, 12); (1, 3, 5, 15); (1, 2, 3, 6, 9, 18); 3
6. (4, 8, 12, 16, 20); (5, 10, 15, 20, 25); 20
7. (3, 6, 9, 12, 15, 18, 21, 24, 27, 30); 10, 20, 30; 30
8. (9, 18, 27, 36, 45); (15, 30, 45); 45
9. (6, 12, 18); (9, 18); 18
10. (8, 16, 24); (12, 24); 24

Unit 9 (p. 49) •••
1. 5   **2.** 4
3. 3   **4.** 12
5. 2   **6.** 3
7. 10   **8.** 2
9. 4   **10.** 63
11. 20   **12.** 15
13. 12   **14.** 18
15. 24   **16.** 24
17. 69   **18.** 42

Unit 9 (p. 50)
Word Problems
1. Every 24 days
2. 32
3. 17
4. Every 12 days
5. 21
6. 84
7. C
8. A

Answer Key • Units 10–12

Unit 10 (p. 52) •
1. 3/8
2. 1/8
3. 6/25
4. 1/8
5. 2
6. 6
7. 9/10
8. 25/6 or 4 1/6

Unit 10 (p. 53) ••
1. 1/6
2. 1/10
3. 1/4
4. 3/8
5. 3/8
6. 3
7. 6
8. 7 1/2
9. 9 1/3
10. 12
11. 3
12. 1 11/16
13. 7/10
14. 5/3
15. 1 13/27
16. 9/2
17. 15 1/2

Unit 10 (p. 54) •••
1. 2/5
2. 1/14
3. 1/8
4. 3/5
5. 1 1/2
6. 4
7. 1 2/5
8. 1 1/2
9. 2 1/2
10. 12 2/3
11. 10
12. 23 3/4
13. 7/12
14. 4
15. 12 1/2
16. 3 3/4
17. 1/7
18. 1 1/2
19. 63 1/3
20. 5 1/4

Unit 10 (p. 55)
Word Problems
1. 1/3
2. 3/8
3. 69
4. 19 13/20
5. 16 1/4
6. 1 3/4
7. C
8. D

Unit 11 (p. 57) •
1. 4
2. 3
3. 2
4. 8
5. 8
6. 6
7. 6
8. 8/9

Unit 11 (p. 58) ••
1. 12
2. 2 1/2
3. 10
4. 4 4/5
5. 10 1/2
6. 12 6/7
7. 1 1/8
8. 7 1/2
9. 6
10. 5 5/9
11. 1 1/9
12. 7 1/5
13. 30
14. 16
15. 1 3/32
16. 1/32
17. 6
18. 7 1/5

Unit 11 (p. 59) •••
1. 6 2/3
2. 9
3. 12 1/2
4. 3 3/7
5. 2 2/5
6. 72
7. 7 1/2
8. 16
9. 4/5
10. 8/9
11. 2 1/4
12. 4 1/2
13. 9/10
14. 3 3/7
15. 4/5
16. 1/2
17. 9
18. 4 6/7
19. 2
20. 7
21. 5 17/20
22. 3 1/6
23. 8 2/3
24. 9 11/21

Unit 11 (p. 60)
Word Problems
1. 12 days
2. 1/4 lb
3. 1 2/5 miles
4. 6 2/13 hours
5. 11 kph
6. 64 slices
7. C
8. C

Unit 12 (p. 62) •
1. 5; −3
2. −4; 4
3. 5; −7
4. +100; −30
5. −2
6. 3, |3|
7. −8, |8|
8. 5, |5|
9. −1, |1|

Unit 12 (p. 63) ••
1. −4
2. 7
3. 20
4. −5
5. −75
6. 150
7. 4
8. 3 |3|
9. −2; |2|
10. 5; |5|
11. −1; |1|
12. 16; |16|
13. −107; |107|
14. 90; |90|

Unit 12 (p. 64) •••
1. 50
2. −20
3. −300
4. −16
5. 1,200; −56
6. 500; 6
7. −9; |9|
8. −8; |8|
9. 94; |94|
10. 2; |2|
11. 15; |15|
12. −72; |72|
13. −200; |200|
14. −60; |60|
15. −19; |19|

Unit 12 (p. 65)
Word Problems
1. −10
2. 2,200
3. −8
4. 45
5. 12
6. 674
7. C
8. C

Common Core Mathematics Grade 6 • ©2012 Newmark Learning, LLC

Answer Key • Units 13–15

1. 5   **2.** 131 and –131
3. –2   **4.** 191 and –191
5. -7   **6.** >
7. <   **8.** >
9. >   **10.** <
11. <   **12.** >
13. >   **14.** >
15. <   **16.** >

1. –1   **2.** –8
3. 151 and –151
4. 27 and –27
5. <   **6.** >
7. >   **8.** >
9. <   **10.** >
11. >   **12.** <
13. <   **14.** >
15. <   **16.** >
17. >   **18.** <
19. >   **20.** <

1. –7   **2.** –84, 84
3. –16   **4.** –252, 252
5. 58   **6.** –9
7. –14, 14   **8.** 8
9. <   **10.** >
11. <   **12.** >
13. <   **14.** <
15. <   **16.** <
17. >   **18.** >
19. >   **20.** >
21. >   **22.** <
23. <   **24.** >

Word Problems
1. A
2. –7, –2, 4, 5
3. C
4. 12, 10, –14, –20
5. B
6. –143, –118, –36, 60, 125
7. B
8. A

Check students' work.

Check students' work.

1. 2, 3   **2.** –4, 3
3. –2, 1   **4.** 4, 1
5. Check students' work.
6. Check students' work.
7. Check students' work.
8. Check students' work.
9. Check students' work.
10. Check students' work.
11. Check students' work.

Word Problems
1. 0, 2
2. J
3. –4, –4
4. 4, 1
5. D
6. A

1. 10^2
2. 10^4
3. 9^2
4. 3^4
5. 6^3
6. 12^1
7. 81
8. 64
9. 243
10. 144
11. 1,000,000
12. 512
13. 400
14. 16

1. 64   **2.** 3 x 3 x 3
3. 2^5, 32   **4.** 5 x 5; 25
5. 6^2; 6 x 6   **6.** 10^3; 1,000
7. 2 x 2 x 2 x 2 x 2; 32
8. 1^6; 1
9. 5^3; 5 x 5 x 5
10. 10 x 10 x 10 x 10 x 10; 100,000
11. 216   **12.** 81
13. 10,000   **14.** 8,000
15. 4,096   **16.** 343
17. 2,500   **18.** 625
19. 4,096   **20.** 27
21. 225   **22.** 32

1. 25   **2.** 6^4; 1,296
3. 8^2, 8 x 8
4. 10 x 10 x 10 x 10 x 10 x 10; 1,000,000
5. 3 x 3 x 3 x 3 x 3 x 3; 729
6. 7^3; 343 **7.** 16^2; 16 x 16
8. 12 x 12 x 12; 1,728
9. 1 x 1 x 1 x 1 x 1 x 1; 1^6
10. 4^3; 64   **11.** 81
12. 64   **13.** 243
14. 144 **15.** 1,000,000
16. 729 **17.** 900
18. 1,296 **19.** 625
20. 6,561 **21.** 10,000
22. 216

Word Problems
1. 20
2. 12
3. 99,000
4. 875
5. 4,032
6. 1,105
7. C
8. D

Answer Key • Units 16–18

Unit 16 (p. 82) •
1. 34
2. 27
3. 25
4. 34
5. 6
6. 8
7. 5
8. 8

Unit 16 (p. 83) ••
1. 24   **2.** 52
3. 8   **4.** 60
5. 29   **6.** 2
7. 68   **8.** 59
9. 12   **10.** 1,250
11. 100   **12.** 4
13. $36 \div (6 - 2) = 9$
14. $6^2 - (3 \times 8) + 2 = 14$
15. $15 - (2 + 5) = 8$

Unit 16 (p. 84) •••
1. 24   **2.** 84
3. 14   **4.** 30
5. 29   **6.** 17
7. 108   **8.** 50
9. 1,100   **10.** 33
11. 81   **12.** 198
13. 75   **14.** 241
15. 2
16. $(7^2 - 17) + 15 = 47$
17. $4 \times (19 - 17) = 2^3$
18. $(5^3 - 9^2) - 3^2 = 35$

Unit 16 (p. 85)
Word Problems
1. 30
2. 206
3. 16
4. 1
5. $(36 \div 6) + (2 \times 13) = 2^5$
6. 24 = 24; true
7. B
8. A

Unit 17 (p. 87) •
1. 6   **2.** 12
3. 24   **4.** 18
5. $n - 5$ **6.** $a \div 3$
7. 16   **8.** 24
9. 42   **10.** 21

Unit 17 (p. 88) ••
1. y **2.** $+ 10$
3. $x \div 15$ **4.** $x - 25$
5. 24   **6.** 18
7. $n - 5$ **8.** $a \div 3$
9. 27   **10.** 7
11. 26   **12.** 28
13. 10   **14.** 20
15. 40   **16.** 40
17. 400

Unit 17 (p. 89) •••
1. $y \div 100$ **2.** $6x$
3. $y - 20$ **4.** $100 \div x$
5. $c + 5^2$ **6.** $x^3 - 56$
7. $n - 12$ **8.** $a \div 5$
9. 80   **10.** 3
11. 32   **12.** 48
13. 4   **14.** 46
15. 12   **16.** 16
17. 1,050

Unit 17 (p. 90)
Word Problems
1. 12
2. 24
3. 25
4. 32
5. 275
6. 366
7. B
8. C

Unit 18 (p. 92) •
1. 12   **2.** 25; 0
3. 14   **4.** 160
5. 25   **6.** 4
7. $6 + 3y$ **8.** $3y$
9. $y + 3$

Unit 18 (p. 93) ••
1. 1   **2.** 9
3. 0   **4.** 28
5. 2   **6.** 9
7. 3   **8.** 64
9. 5   **10.** 45
11. 5   **12.** 6
13. $8a + 6b = 74$
14. $12b - 8a = 52$
15. $8a - 4b = 4$
16. $(10a + 2b) \div c = 27$

Unit 18 (p. 94) •••
1. 1   **2.** 7
3. 0   **4.** 27
5. 16   **6.** 8
7. 22   **8.** 7
9. 6   **10.** 7
11. 12   **12.** 11
13. 7   **14.** 13
15. 6
16. $(a + b + c) \times 5 = 55$
17. $7ab - 2ac = 16$
18. $8a - 4b = -8$
19. $4 \times (b + c) \div a = 40$
20. $2 \times (4 + b) \times c = 96$

Unit 18 (p. 95)
Word Problems
1. 5
2. 8
3. 6
4. true
5. $5v + 30$
6. $4(2a - 3b)$
7. C
8. A

Answer Key • Units 19–22

Unit 19 (p. 97) •
1. $n + 8 = 10$
2. $n \div 12 = 10$
3. $8n - 6 = 34$
4. $3(n + 12) = 45$
5. yes
6. no
7. no
8. yes
9. 36
10. 168

Unit 19 (p. 98) ••
1. $n + 6 = 10$
2. $n - 50 = 16$
3. $n \times 10 + 5 = 65$
4. $(16 \div s) - 3 = 5$
5. $6(n + 4) = 54$
6. yes
7. yes
8. no
9. no
10. yes
11. yes
12. 48   13. 65

Unit 19 (p. 99) •••
1. $n + 6 = 15$
2. $n \div 15 = 4$
3. $7 \times 30 = n$
4. $270 \div x = 90$
5. $3y + 45 = 95$
6. $3(n + 12) = 45$
7. yes   8. yes
9. no   10. yes
11. yes   12. no
13. yes   14. no
15. yes   16. 225
17. 72   18. 275

Unit 19 (p. 100)
Word Problems
1. $y - 25 = 100$
2. $n + 25 = 100; n = 75$
3. $y = 77$
4. $s = 5$
5. $g = 3$
6. $r = 6$
7. D
8. C

Unit 20 (p. 102) •
1. >
2. <
3. $n \times 6 > 11$
4. $n + 4 < 10$
5. 6, 7   6. 2, 1
7. 7, 8, 9
8. 3, 2, 1

Unit 20 (p. 103) ••
1. $n < 10$
2. $n + 5 > 10$
3. $p > 40$ 4. $x < 16$
5. $2y < 15$
6. $c \div 3 < 20$ 7. 8, 9
8. 4, 5   9. 7, 8, 9
10. 4, 5, 6

Unit 20 (p. 104) •••
1. $y > 50$ 2. $n + 9 > 20$
3. $x < 15$ 4. $n - 5 < 10$
5. $5n > 10$ 6. $c \div 4 < 25$
7. 3, 4, 5   8. 3, 2, 1
9. 2, 1, 0   10. 6, 7, 8

Unit 20 (p. 105)
Word Problems
1. $n < 50$
2. $n > 5$
3. $n < 100$
4. $n > 32$
5. $n < 60$ 6. $n > 2$
7. C   8. D

Unit 21 (p. 107) •
Check students' work.
1. $y = 4, 3, 2$
2. $y = 3, 2, 1, 0$
3. $D = 20, 25$

Unit 21 (p. 108) ••
Check students' work.
1. $y = 9, 7, 5, 3$
2. $y = 4, 3, 2, 1$
3. $c = 8, 10, 12, 14$

Unit 21 (p. 109) •••
Check students' work.
1. $y = 10, 8, 6, 4, 2$
2. $y = 7, 5, 3, 1, -1$
3. $D = 60, 90, 120, 150$

Unit 21 (p. 110)
Word Problems
1. 0, 2
2. $y = x + 2$
3. $y = 8$
4. $y = 5, 4, 3, 2$
5. D
6. A

Unit 22 (p. 112) •
1. 20 sq units
2. 6 sq units
3. 10 sq units
4. 18 sq units
5. 2 sq m
6. 32 sq ft

Unit 22 (p. 113) ••
1. 18 sq units
2. 35 sq m
3. 35 sq units
4. 12 sq units
5. 9 sq units
6. 10 sq m
7. 24 sq cm
8. 4.5 sq ft

Unit 22 (p. 114) •••
1. 18 sq units
2. 35 sq m
3. 45 sq ft
4. 30 sq m
5. 32 m^2 6. 25 mm^2
7. 2 yd^2 8. 30 cm^2
9. 72 cm^2
10. 200 mm^2

Unit 22 (p. 115)
Word Problems
1. 40 sq in
2. 25 sq cm
3. 144 sq ft
4. 40 sq cm
5. 350 sq in
6. 42 sq cm
7. A
8. C

Answer Key • Units 23–26

Unit 23 (p. 117) •
Check students' work.
1. parallelogram
2. triangle
3. (–5, –6)
4. Answers will vary.

Unit 23 (p. 118) ••
Check students' work.
1. trapezoid
2. rectangle
3. (–3, –4), (–3, –8)
4. Answers will vary.

Unit 23 (p. 119) •••
Check students' work.
1. parallelogram
2. triangle
3. (–1, –2), (–1, –6)
4. Answers will vary.
5. Answers will vary.

Unit 23 (p. 120)
Word Problems
1. (–8, 5), (–3, 5), (–2, –3), (–7, –3)
2. Triangle EFG
3. Answers will vary.
4. (3, –3), (7, –6), (4, –8)
5. B   6. D

Unit 24 (p. 122) •
1. Check students' work.
2. Check students' work.
3. Check students' work.
4. 150 sq cm
5. 24 sq cm

Unit 24 (p. 123) ••
1. 52 sq m
2. 96 sq cm
3. 54 sq m
4. 64 sq cm
5. 384 sq m
6. 76 sq in
7. 18 sq ft

Unit 24 (p. 124) •••
1. 208 sq m
2. 288 sq cm
3. 260 sq cm
4. 486 sq m
5. 37.5 sq m
6. 148 sq cm
7. 76 sq cm
8. 115 sq cm

Unit 24 (p. 125)
Word Problems
1. 222 sq in
2. 656 sq in
3. 70 sq ft
4. 96 sq in
5. B
6. A

Unit 25 (p. 127) •
1. 28 units^3
2. 62.4 cm^3
3. 125 m^3
4. 54.4 ft^3
5. 42 7/8 in^3

Unit 25 (p. 128) ••
1. 108 units^3
2. 75.6 in^3
3. 70 ft^3
4. 28 cm^3
5. 97.5 m^3
6. 166.375 in^3
7. 232.8 ft^3
8. 421.875 in^3
9. 181.5 ft^3

Unit 25 (p. 129) •••
1. 55.69 m^3 2. 34.33 in^3
3. 86.33 ft^3 4. 91.46 in^3
5. 140 in^3 6. 75.6 in^3
7. 43.56 cm^3 8. 107.6 m^3
9. 12.17 ft^3 10. 270.51 cm^3
11. 1,423.83 in^3 12. 98 ft^3

Unit 25 (p. 130)
Word Problems
1. 4 1/4 ft^3
2. 63 ft^3
3. 561 1/8 in^3
4. 0.5 m^3
5. 240,000 mL
6. 205 m^3
7. D
8. C

Unit 26 (p. 132) •
1. 86
2. 28
3. 86
4. 6
5. 3
6. 25 and 30

Unit 26 (p. 133) ••
1. $37; $35
2. 1; 0.75
3. 19.1; 19.5
4. 21; 22
5. 88; 89
6. 2.3; 2
7. 19
8. 3.75, 4.25
9. $27; $26; $25
10. $216.33; $209; none

Unit 26 (p. 134) •••
1. 79; 80; none
2. 93; 92; 92
3. 84; 85; none
4. 89; 88; 88
5. 1; 0.5; 0.25
6. 94.75; 95.5; 96
7. 8.7; 8.5; 8
8. 3; 3; 2.5
9. 33.4; 34; none
10. 1.75; 1, none

Unit 26 (p. 135)
Word Problems
1. 84.5
2. 40
3. 40 minutes
4. 98
5. 18
6. 1.1
7. B
8. C

    Common Core Mathematics Grade 6 • ©2012 Newmark Learning, LLC

Answer Key • Units 27–29

Unit 27 (p. 137) •
Check students' work.
1. 2
2. 15
3. 2
4. 2
5. 2
6. 4

Unit 27 (p. 138) ••
Check students' work.
1. 15
2. 5
3. 1
4. 1
5. Check students' work.
6. 3
7. 2
8. 15
9. 2

Unit 27 (p. 139) •••
Check students' work.
1. 6
2. 10
3. 10
4. the mode; because most students spend 10 hours studying each week
5. 2
6. 2
7. 3
8. 5
9. 2.5
10. the mode; because most students study 2 hours a night

Unit 27 (p. 140)
Word Problems
Check students' work.
1. 80–86; 6
2. 83
3. 84
4. 4
5. 3, 4, and 5
6. 4
7. C
8. C

Unit 28 (p. 142) •
Check students' work.
1. 5
2. range of 10 pounds
3. 23
4. 69
5. 41–50

Unit 28 (p. 143) ••
Check students' work.
1. 150
2. 650
3. 2–4 p.m.
4. 8 hr
5. 1–10
6. 41–50
7. 69
8. 1–10 and 61–70

Unit 28 (p. 144) •••
Check students' work.
1. range of 10 pounds
2. 22
3. 39
4. 11–20
5. 300
6. 1,350
7. 4–6 p.m.
8. 12 hr

Unit 28 (p. 145)
Word Problems
Check students' work.
1. 39
2. 81–90
3. 61–70
4. 18
5. 3
6. 15
7. B
8. A

Unit 29 (p. 147) •
Check students' work.
1. 91
2. 128
3. 105
4. 98
5. 117
6. 19

Unit 29 (p. 148) ••
Check students' work.
1. 5, 18, 20, 25, 27, 35, 38, 40, 48, 60, 90
2. Check students' work.
3. 35
4. 20
5. 48
6. 35
7. 20 and 48 (Answers may vary.)
8. 28

Unit 29 (p. 149) •••
Check students' work.
1. 63
2. 100
3. 88
4. 75
5. 94
6. 19
7. 75 and 94 (Answers may vary.)
8. 37

Unit 29 (p. 150)
Word Problems
Check students' work.
1. 36
2. 57
3. 45
4. 40
5. 48
6. 8
7. A
8. C

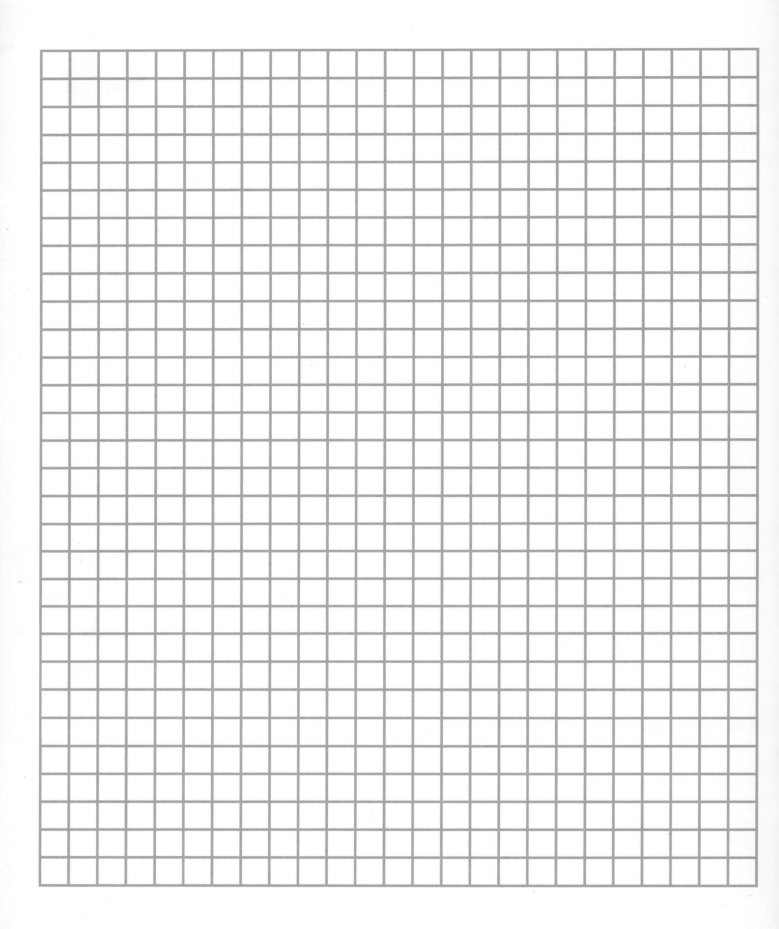

160